Understanding Networks

E. Joseph Guay
Fleet Services
Bryant College

West Publishing Company
Minneapolis/St. Paul ♦ New York ♦ Los Angeles ♦ San Francisco

WEST'S COMMITMENT TO THE ENVIRONMENT

In 1906, West Publishing Company began recycling materials left over from the production of books. This began a tradition of efficient and responsible use of resources. Today, up to 95% of our legal books and 70% of our college and school texts are printed on recycled, acid-free stock. West also recycles nearly 22 million pounds of scrap paper annually—the equivalent of 181,717 trees. Since the 1960s, West has devised ways to capture and recycle waste inks, solvents, oils, and vapors created in the printing process. We also recycle plastics of all kinds, wood, glass, corrugated cardboard, and batteries, and have eliminated the use of styrofoam book packaging. We at West are proud of the longevity and the scope of our commitment to the environment.

Production, Prepress, Printing and Binding by West Publishing Company

Production Management by Lisa M. Labrecque

 Printed on 10% Post Consumer Recycled Paper

Netware is a registered trademark of Novell, Inc.

DECConnect is a registered trademark of DEC Corporation.

Windows NT and DOS are registered trademarks of Microsoft Corporation.

IBM, IBM personal computer, and IBM PC are registered trademarks of International Business Machines Corporation.

Library of Congress Cataloging-in-Publication Data

Guay, E. Joseph.
    Understanding networks / E. Joseph Guay.
        p.   cm. -- (The Microcomputing series)
    Includes index.
    ISBN 0-314-01350-4 (soft)
    1. Computer networks.   I. Title.   II. Series.
TK5105.5.G83   1994
004.6'8--dc20
                                      93-13517
                                        CIP

Contents

Publisher's Note

This book is part of THE MICROCOMPUTING SERIES. This popular series provides the most comprehensive list of books dealing with microcomputer applications software. We have expanded the number of software topics and provided a flexible set of instructional materials for all courses. This unique series includes five different types of books.

1. *West's Microcomputing Custom Editions* give instructors the power to create a spiral-bound microcomputer applications book especially for their course. Instructors can select the applications they want to teach and the amount of material they want to cover for each application—essentials or intermediate length. The following titles are available for the 1994 Microcomputing Series custom editions program:

   Understanding Information Systems

   Understanding Networks

   DOS (3.x) and System

   DOS 5 and System

   DOS 6 and System

   Windows 3.0

   Windows 3.1

   WordPerfect 5.0

   WordPerfect 5.1

   WordPerfect 6.0

   WordPerfect for Windows (Release 5.1 and 5.2)

   Microsoft Word for Windows Version 1.1

   Microsoft Word for Windows Version 2.0

PageMaker 4

Lotus 1-2-3 Release 2.01

Lotus 1-2-3 Release 2.2

Lotus 1-2-3 Release 2.3

Lotus 1-2-3 Release 2.4

Lotus 1-2-3 Release 3

Lotus 1-2-3 for Windows Release 4

Microsoft Excel 3

Microsoft Excel 4

Quattro Pro 4

Quattro Pro for Windows

dBASE III Plus

dBASE IV Version 1.0 / 1.1 / 1.5

dBASE IV Version 2.0

Paradox 3.5

Paradox for Windows

Microsoft Access

For more information about *West's Microcomputing Custom Editions*, please contact your local West Representative, or call West Publishing Company at 512-327-3175.

2. General concepts books for teaching basic hardware and software philosophy and applications are available separately or in combination with hands-on applications. These books provide students with a general overview of computer fundamentals including history, social issues, and a synopsis of software and hardware applications. These books include *Understanding Information Systems,* by Steven C. Ross.

3. A series of hands-on laboratory tutorials (*Understanding and Using*) are software specific and cover a wide range of individual packages. These tutorials, written at an introductory level, combine tutorials with complete reference guides. A complete list of series titles can be found on the following pages.

4. Several larger volumes combining DOS with three application software packages are available in different combinations. These texts are titled *Understanding and Using Application Software*. They condense components of the individual lab manuals and add conceptual coverage for courses that require both software tutorials and microcomputer concepts in a single volume.

5. A series of advanced-level, hands-on lab manuals provide students with a strong project/systems orientation. These include *Understanding and Using Lotus 1-2-3: Advanced Techniques Releases 2.2 and 2.3*, by Judith C. Simon.

THE MICROCOMPUTING SERIES has been successful in providing you with a full range of applications books to suit your individual needs. We remain committed to excellence in offering the widest variety of current software packages. In addition, we are committed to producing microcomputing texts that provide you both the coverage you desire and also the level and format most appropriate for your students. The Acquisitions Editor of the series is Rick Leyh of West Educational Publishing; the Consulting Editor is Steve Ross of Western Washington University. We are always planning for the future in this series. Please send us your comments and suggestions:

Rick Leyh
West Educational Publishing
1515 Capital of Texas Highway South
Suite 402
Austin, Texas 78746

Steve Ross
Associate Professor/MIS
College of Business and Economics
Western Washington University
Bellingham, Washington 98225
Electronic Mail: STEVEROSS@WWU.EDU

We now offer these books in THE MICROCOMPUTING SERIES:

General Concepts

Understanding Information Systems
by Steven C. Ross

Understanding Computer Information Systems
by Paul W. Ross, H. Paul Haiduk, H. Willis Means; and Robert B. Sloger

**Operating Systems/
Environments**

Understanding and Using Microsoft Windows 3.1
by Steven C. Ross and Ronald W. Maestas

Understanding and Using Microsoft Windows 3.0
by Steven C. Ross and Ronald W. Maestas

Understanding and Using MS-DOS 6.0
by Jonathan P. Bacon

Understanding and Using MS-DOS/PC DOS 5.0
by Jonathan P. Bacon

Understanding and Using MS-DOS/PC DOS 4.0
by Jonathan P. Bacon

Networks

Understanding Networks
by E. Joseph Guay

Word Processors

Understanding and Using WordPerfect for Windows
by Jonathan P. Bacon

Understanding and Using Microsoft Word for Windows 2.0
by Larry Lozuk and Emily M. Ketcham

Understanding and Using Microsoft Word for Windows (1.1)
by Larry Lozuk

Understanding and Using WordPerfect 6.0
by Jonathan P. Bacon

Understanding and Using WordPerfect 5.1
by Jonathan P. Bacon and Cody T. Copeland

Understanding and Using WordPerfect 5.0
by Patsy H. Lund

Desktop Publishing

Understanding and Using PageMaker 4
by John R. Nicholson

**Spreadsheet
Software**

Understanding and Using Quattro Pro for Windows
by Larry D. Smith

Understanding and Using Microsoft Excel 4
by Steven C. Ross and Stephen V. Hutson

Understanding and Using Microsoft Excel 3
by Steven C. Ross and Stephen V. Hutson

Understanding and Using Lotus 1-2-3 for Windows Release 4
by Steven C. Ross and Alan H. Bauld

Understanding and Using Quattro Pro 4
by Steven C. Ross and Stephen V. Hutson

Understanding and Using Lotus 1-2-3 Release 2.01
by Steven C. Ross

Understanding and Using Lotus 1-2-3 Release 2.2
by Steven C. Ross

Understanding and Using Lotus 1-2-3 Release 2.3 and Release 2.4
by Steven C. Ross

Understanding and Using Lotus 1-2-3 Release 3
by Steven C. Ross

Understanding and Using Lotus 1-2-3: Advanced Techniques Releases 2.2 and 2.3
by Judith C. Simon

Database Management Software

Understanding and Using Microsoft Access
by Bruce J. McLaren

Understanding and Using Paradox for Windows
by Larry D. Smith

Understanding and Using Paradox 3.5
by Larry D. Smith

Understanding and Using dBASE III Plus, 2nd Edition
by Steven C. Ross

Understanding and Using dBASE IV Version 2.0
by Steven C. Ross

Understanding and Using dBASE IV
by Steven C. Ross

Integrated Software

Understanding and Using Microsoft Works 3.0 for the PC
by Gary Bitter

Understanding and Using Microsoft Works 3.0 for the Macintosh
by Gary Bitter

Understanding and Using ClarisWorks
by Gary Bitter

Understanding and Using Microsoft Works 2.0 on the Macintosh
by Gary Bitter

Understanding and Using Microsoft Works 2.0 on the IBM PC
by Gary Bitter

Combined Books

Essentials of Application Software, Volume 1: DOS, WordPerfect 5.0/5.1, Lotus 1-2-3 Release 2.2, dBASE III Plus
by Steven C. Ross, Jonathan P. Bacon, and Cody T. Copeland

Understanding and Using Application Software, Volume 4: DOS, WordPerfect 5.0, Lotus 1-2-3 Release 2, dBASE IV
by Patsy H. Lund, Jonathan P. Bacon, and Steven C. Ross

Understanding and Using Application Software, Volume 5: DOS, WordPerfect 5.0/5.1, Lotus 1-2-3 Release 2.2, dBASE III Plus
by Steven C. Ross, Jonathan P. Bacon, and Cody T. Copeland

Advanced Books

Understanding and Using Lotus 1-2-3: Advanced Techniques Releases 2.2 and 2.3
by Judith C. Simon

Understanding Networks

Preface

As the title implies, this book is meant to be an introduction to both the concepts behind local area networks (LANs) and their practical uses. It grew out of an eight-week course and a two-day seminar that I designed and presented several times over a three-year period from 1990 to 1992 at the Center for Management Development at Bryant College, Smithfield, Rhode Island. My approach was to present the concepts and theories in a standard classroom or conference room setting, provide tours of LAN installations, and conduct hands-on sessions in a computerized classroom equipped with a LAN. Approximately 40 percent of the time was in the classroom, 5 percent on tours of LAN installations, and 55 percent in hands-on sessions or demonstrations with a LAN. Although the materials focus on PC systems and Novell Netware, the concepts translate easily to other types of networks.

This material has been presented to a wide range of students, including undergraduate information system majors, accounting majors, computer center staff and managers, office workers, people contemplating a career change, information workers wanting to learn more about LANs, and mixtures of these. It can be regarded as an overview course for the nonspecialist and an introductory course for the student who wishes to focus on networking; I have successfully presented it to a class with a mixture of these two types of students. The common denominator is to help the student come to a better understanding of the capabilities and shortcomings of LAN technology and to appreciate the role that LANs have played in the rapid evolution of information systems. An important aspect of this book is its practical side, since it shows how to set up a LAN and presents the details of managing a Novell network.

Although this text is not meant to be a "how-to" guide, it does cover many technical points in setting up and using LANs and includes hands-on exercises that can be valuable aids in understanding networks. Enough background information on DOS and PC hardware is included in the first units to allow readers without a strong computing background to proceed through the networking portion.

The materials covered in this book are accurate and current to the best of my knowledge and are based on extensive experience with setting up, testing, and managing scores of LAN configurations. The material is organized into units that present related concepts in a standard format that is easy for the student to digest. Each unit is mostly self-contained to provide flexibility in choosing what is to be covered.

About the Author

The author has more than 15 years of teaching experience in higher education and has designed and taught courses and seminars on local area networks. He is a Certified Netware Engineer and Certified Netware Instructor and has professionally installed, configured and managed more than 15 LANs and has professionally evaluated and tested scores of LAN configurations.

Unit 1 **LAN Concepts**

Learning Objectives

At the completion of this unit, you should be able to

1. understand what a local area network is,
2. identify the main components of a LAN,
3. describe the most important capabilities of a LAN,
4. appreciate the uses of a LAN in an office environment.

The Elements of a Local Area Network

Simply stated, a **local area network** (LAN) is a group of personal computers (PCs) or workstations linked in such a way as to permit them to share software applications and information, use mass storage (hard disks), and share peripheral equipment such as printers.

An essential element of a LAN is the capability to instantly connect authorized users with all available resources.

Components of a Local Area Network

Every LAN must have some type of connection between computers and some kind of software system to facilitate communication. The following components are typical of *most* LANs.

➡ A **network file server** provides network users with such resources as disk sharing and printing. In most networks, a PC or proprietary device is dedicated for exclusive use as a server. In some networks, any PC can provide such services, while others use a minicomputer or UNIX **workstation** to provide them.

➡ A **network operating system** runs on the server and enables it to provide network resources. The operating system could be a general purpose one such as UNIX or OS/2 that has components to provide network services, or it may be a specialized one such as Novell Netware dedicated to providing network services.

➡ A **network interface card (NIC)** is the component that goes into a PC or workstation and enables it to communicate with other resources on the network. Types of cards include Token Ring, Ethernet, Starlan, and Arcnet. The cost of an interface card can range from less than $100 to more than $800, depending on the technology, performance, and computer interface for which it is designed.

➡ **Workstation software** includes the local operating system and any additional software necessary to communicate with resources on the network. Some systems, like the Macintosh, have network capabilities built in. Others, like DOS, require additional software to communicate on the network. This additional software is often called a **shell** because it constitutes an outside layer between the operating system and the network.

➡ A **wire** gives network workstations a means of transmitting a signal to each other. Some networks are wireless, while some use fiber optics, but the vast majority use some type of copper wire. Wire comes in several varieties, but the most common is twisted pair and resembles standard telephone wire.

➡ A **network wiring hub** is, as the name implies, a central "junction box" for the wiring that goes to each workstation on the network. The hub can also provide important resources for managing and troubleshooting network malfunctions.

➡ A **backup device** can be used to store a copy of network data in the event of a system malfunction. The most common type of backup device uses a tape cassette to store anywhere from 100 to 1,000 megabytes of data.

➡ A standby or uninterruptable power supply (**UPS**) is a special power supply that normally is placed between the server and the AC outlet. It can provide power to the server in the event of a general power failure. Normally, a UPS provides power only for enough time to enable the server to perform housekeeping tasks and be shut down in a normal fashion. This greatly reduces the chances of massive data loss.

Functions of a LAN

As a connectivity tool, a LAN functions primarily to provide access to data, printers, or other computing resources in the organization. Here are some specific examples:

Sharing Printers

A LAN can provide easy access to printers. This capability is especially useful for large, high-speed printers or specialized devices such as PostScript printers for desktop publishing. In most LANs a shared printer can be set up so that it appears to be a local printer as far as the PC software is concerned. This makes it possible to use a shared printer without making special modifications to the PC software.

The LAN may also use a PC or other device to act as a **print server**. The print server takes care of the task of printing on a network by accepting print output from network users and sending print jobs to the appropriate network printer. A print server must be able to handle the task of managing multiple print requests going to different network printers.

Providing Mass Storage

Another common use of a LAN is to provide large amounts of disk storage. Because large drives are generally less costly per megabyte than smaller drives, their use in a network server can provide a cost-effective way to provide **mass storage** to network users. At the same time, the network disk drive can be set up so that it can be used much like a local hard disk drive.

Sharing Data

One of the most important features of a LAN is the capability to permit many users to have nearly simultaneous access to information stored on shared mass storage. Central storage of data can allow all authorized users to have accurate and up-to-date information. If one user updates the information, all the others will have immediate access to the changes. Of course, the network operating system and software must provide a means to ensure that the changes are made in an orderly fashion.

Some networks provide software and hardware specially devoted to the task of providing database services. A **database server** can be a dedicated system, or it can be a service provided by the network file server. Most database servers respond to a specialized database query language such as Structured Query Language (**SQL**).

Providing Network Security

In most situations, the network must be able to restrict access to sensitive data or resources to only authorized users. This **network security** is yet another task of the network operating system.

Providing Communication Services

A LAN is a communication system, and as such it can provide a variety of services, including connecting to mainframe computers, sending faxes, or transmitting electronic mail around the campus or across the country. In fact, electronic mail, or **E-mail**, is one of the most popular and useful services provided by a network.

Sharing Software

Most popular software is now available in special network versions that allow simultaneous use by more than one station on the network. The purchase of a network license can be more cost-effective than purchase of individual copies of software for each user, and it can also provide a significant management advantage, in that the software need not be installed (or upgraded) for each user.

Facilitating Group Interaction

A new category of programs called **groupware** is specially designed to take advantage of the unique communication capabilities of a network. This evolving class of software can enhance communication and interaction among the members of a group or team. For example, a calendar and scheduling package could provide the capability to automatically determine when the members of a committee are free to meet. Another program could allow a team to collaborate efficiently on the writing of a manual or user's guide. Another might enhance the development of new ideas by providing an ongoing forum for exchanging observations and comments. Lotus Notes is an example of a recent software product that falls into the groupware category.

Permitting Distributed Processing across the Network

Networks provide the capability to "farm out" or distribute processing chores to resources on the network. For example, a database server can provide rapid network access to large stores of information. When an application has been implemented to use this type of service, it can send out a query or data request over the network to the database server. The server performs any necessary data extraction and formatting, then sends the results back to the requesting application. This can happen without the knowledge or intervention of the user.

The **distributed processing** approach to providing resources offers many advantages. Specialized devices such as database servers can be optimized to carry out specific chores efficiently, thus providing more effective services to network users. For example, the database server can provide users with more rapid access to data, relieve the local system of this processing task, and reduce the level of traffic on a network.

Enhancing Software Support and Training

Networks can also be used to enhance software support and staff training. For example, a network can be used to enable a user services staff person to see and "remotely control" another system. This can greatly enhance the efficiency of software support by making it unnecessary for the support person to be in the same place as the user.

A LAN can be used in a classroom to broadcast a computer image from the instructor's station to all in the class. This can provide an alternative to a large-screen projector.

Linking Networks

Bridges, **routers**, and **gateways** are specialized components that provide interconnections between a LAN and another LAN or **wide area network** (WAN). Bridges serve to link two similar networks together, while routers provide additional translation and route selection features for more complex networks. Not only can a router link two or more LANs together, but it can also act as "gatekeeper" between the LANs to isolate local traffic. A gateway is the most complex of the devices, linking dissimilar networks.

Evolving Importance of LANs

Since the introduction of time-sharing systems, there has been a significant evolution in the ways that resources are used and shared. The minicomputer was a success because it gave users easier access to central processing power. PCs have been successful largely because they are easy to use and they deliver independent processing power to the desktop.

LANs have been successful because they can provide the best of both the timesharing and the PC worlds. A workstation or PC on a LAN can deliver processing power to the desktop while also providing access to shared data, mass storage, and printing resources on the network. A LAN can also provide office automation services such as electronic mail.

Role of a LAN

The exact role of a LAN in a given organization will depend on the details of its information processing environment. If a central computer and a variety of stand-alone PCs are present, a local area network can link the PC users to the central system, while also providing the usual range of LAN resources. A departmental LAN can also offload some of the functions of the central system that are specific to that department.

If there is no central computer, a local area network based on a central file and print server can provide much of the functionality of a central computer system.

Comparing a LAN to a Minicomputer

While a properly designed LAN can be an alternative to a minicomputer system, there are some important differences.

Relative Maturity

The minicomputer has reached technological maturity, with many existing applications and relatively high levels of experience.

In contrast, LAN technology is comparatively new. As a result, a LAN can be less reliable and more difficult to manage. In addition, not all software packages have been adapted for use on a LAN. However, the rate of development of new LAN applications has exploded and the level of user experience is growing rapidly.

Cost-Effectiveness

When compared to a minicomputer or mainframe, a LAN can be very cost-effective, especially if there are a number of PCs already installed in an organization.

Expandability

A LAN can be expanded extensively without major hardware changes. This is true for two reasons. First, each new system on the LAN contains a microprocessor that provides more computing power to serve the additional user. While it is true that the demands on the central file server also increase with each new user, the increase is a relatively small one. Second, if the network expands to the point that one file server is no longer adequate to meet the needs, another file server can be added, the network divided into logical subnetworks, and applications transferred while still using the original server. In many cases, the expanded network can be brought on-line with no downtime at all. This makes a LAN quite easy to expand in small increments.

In contrast, each new station added to a minicomputer or mainframe also adds proportionately more of a load for the central processor. This often results in degradation of performance as each new user is added. At some point, a major upgrade of the central system is required.

LANs and the Evolution of Computing Power

Astonishingly, the personal computer of today contains the computing power of mainframes built less than a decade ago. Personal computers continue to become more powerful and capable of running greatly more sophisticated software and operating systems. As PCs continue to evolve, they will place more useful resources on the desktop. Computers that use graphical interfaces and powerful operating systems like UNIX, OS/2, and Windows NT are becoming more common in the business world and may someday be the dominant desktop systems. Networking capabilities are already integrated into these operating systems.

The local area network can provide the "glue" to join PCs, workstations, minicomputers, and mainframes so that users can have access to the resources they need. As more LAN-specific software is developed, the LAN will provide capabilities that are not available with traditional time-sharing systems. Networks are evolving to provide increased capabilities for distributed processing to the extent that in some organizations the network itself has become more important even than the large central system.

Summary

A LAN usually consists of some type of wiring, network interface cards, a wiring hub, plus a server, and uses an operating system such as UNIX or Novell Netware to make these services available. A local area network can provide shared access to printers, mass storage, data, and other resources.

The number of LANs is increasing rapidly and, once installed, a LAN tends to grow as users see the benefits. LANs are rapidly becoming an important part of the information systems infrastructure. The initial challenges of getting the LAN installed and operating properly are giving way to problems of managing the network and keeping up with the demand for new services.

The rapid growth of networking is an indication of its importance in the evolution of information systems. Many organizations view networking as an important tool for workgroup productivity, and, hence, a means of obtaining an advantage over the competition. For a small organization, a LAN can provide the basis of a company information system. For a large organization, a LAN can be an integral part of the corporate information system, providing the ability to connect to mainframe systems and to communicate with corporate users at other locations.

Ultimately, networks and information systems will be closely integrated and tasks will be sent over the network to the resource that is most appropriate for carrying out the job. This will be done without special action on the part of the end user.

Review Questions

The answers to questions marked by an asterisk are in Appendix B.

1. List the major hardware and software components of a LAN.
2. Name some of the major functions of a LAN.
* 3. What do the following acronyms and terms mean?
    a. NIC
    b. WAN
    c. Hub

Exercises

1. Sketch a diagram showing the main components and the layout of a LAN as it relates or might relate to an organization with which you are familiar. Indicate who is or who would be connected, where a central server is or might be located, and where wiring could be placed.

2. List the two or three most important LAN functions in your environment or in an environment with which you are familiar.

3. If you want to select a subset of information from a data set that is stored on a network file server, the data is sent over the network and the selection is done on the local PC. Detail how this differs from the way a subset of data is extracted by a database server.

Key Terms

The following terms are introduced in this unit. Be sure that you know what each of them means.

Backup device

Bridge

Database server

Distributed processing

E-mail

Gateway

Groupware

Local area network

Mass storage

Network file server

Network interface card (NIC)

Network operating system

Network security

Network wiring hub

Print server

Router

Shell

SQL

UPS

Wide area network

Wire

Workstation

Workstation software

Unit 2 **PC Hardware**

Most local area networks consist of personal computers linked in such a way that they can communicate and share resources. Most network file servers are high-powered personal computers. Thus, an understanding of PC systems is a prerequisite to understanding most local area networks. In this unit, we review some hardware aspects of PCs that are important in networking.

Learning Objectives

At the completion of this unit, you should be able to

1. identify the main components of a PC,
2. understand the most important computer hardware terms,
3. determine the features of a PC that are required for your needs,
4. understand the special hardware requirements for a network file server.

Components of a Typical PC

A typical personal computer, as shown in Figure 2-1, includes a **keyboard**, **monitor**, and **system unit**, housing the **microprocessor** that serves as the central processing unit (**CPU**). The system unit also contains **system memory**, one or more floppy drives, and usually a hard disk drive that provides mass storage. It may also contain one or more **add-in cards** to provide additional capabilities. For example, an add-in card is usually required to provide networking capabilities.

Monitor and Video Adapter

In general, PC video and graphics capabilities can vary considerably and are related to the type of monitor and **video adapter** used. Displays (monitors) can be classified according to color capabilities (monochrome or color), type of interface (digital or analog), and the amount of detail they can show (usually indicated by the number of

Figure 2-1
Components of a Personal
Computer

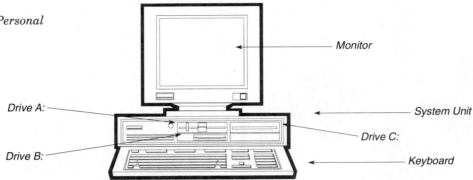

dots per inch of horizontal and vertical resolution). Typical combinations are:

MDA	Monochrome, TTL (digital), 720×350
Hercules	Same as MDA with graphics capabilities
CGA	Color, TTL, 640×200
EGA	Color, TTL, 640×350
VGA	Color, analog, 640×480
Super VGA	Color, analog, 800×600 or 1,024×768
XGA, 8514	Color, analog, 1,024×768, 1,280×1,024

The type of video adapter can affect the way your computer uses system memory and, hence, can also affect your setup options for using your system on a LAN.

Microprocessor

The microprocessor is the "brain" of the computer and is able to carry out millions of program instructions per second. The Intel family of microprocessors used in most IBM-compatible PCs are classified according to the type and clock speed. Processor types include the 8086, 8088, 286, 386SX, 386, 486SX, 486, 586 (Pentium), and 686. (It is common practice to abbreviate 80286 to 286, 80386 to 386, and so on.) There are significant limitations in the 8086 and 286 processors as compared with the 386SX and later types. Clock speeds range from under 5MHz to 50MHz or more. (MHz is an abbreviation of megahertz which stands for millions of cycles per second.)

Even within the 386 and 486 family there is a relatively wide range of capabilities. The 386SX processor is at the low end. This processor is internally the same as the 386 (or 386DX) but instead of a 32-bit address and data bus, it uses 24 bits for addresses and 16 bits for data (this is the same type of external addressing as the 286 processor). Clock speeds commonly range from 16 to 25MHz. The 486 processor includes a second processor for math operations (a math coprocessor) and a program cache that helps it anticipate instructions. (The 486SX does not include the math coprocessor.) The 486 also comes in a DX2 version that operates internally at twice the speed as the external bus. For example, the 486DX2/66 operates internally at 66MHz and externally at 33MHz.

Processing Speed

The processing speed is an indication of how fast a computer will run a particular application and is sometimes measured in units of millions of instructions per second, or **MIPS**. The type of processor and the clock speed are the most important factors in determining the actual MIPS rating of a computer. However, other factors such as the speed of the graphics adapter, the speed of mass storage, and the design of the computer also affect the actual speed when running a specific application. A 386DX/33 (a 386DX running at 33MHz) may be twice as fast as a 386SX/25, while a 486SX/25 about 25 percent faster than the 386/33, and a 486DX2/66 five to eight times faster than the 486SX/25. The 586 (Pentium) processor is about four times faster than the 486 processor.

Graphic Coprocessor

Because of the popularity of Windows, some vendors are offering graphic coprocessors and integrated graphic adapters designed to speed the performance of systems while running Windows. Some systems also include a high-speed "local bus" between the processor and the video adapter.

System Memory

The unit of system memory is the **byte**, which is 8 **bits** (binary digits) and is the amount of memory used to store a text character. System memory is normally expressed in terms of 1 **kilobyte** (KB) = 1,024 bytes, or 1 **megabyte** (MB) = 1,024KB.

Most computers are equipped with at least 640KB of system memory, which is the amount that DOS can use effectively. Although DOS can address 1MB of memory, the memory addresses between 640KB and 1,024KB are usually reserved for use by peripheral devices such as the display adapter or network interface adapters. This memory is called high memory or **high RAM**.

XMS Memory

Since DOS can use up to 640KB of system memory, 640KB or 1MB is considered the minimum amount of memory for a network PC. This is because the network software uses up part of the available memory. Beyond this, it is common to find 386SX systems equipped with 2MB or more of memory and 386/486 systems equipped with 4MB or more. The additional memory is particularly useful in a 386- or 486-based computer because it can be used by programs such as Windows and OS/2 to further improve system performance. Memory beyond 1MB is called extended memory or **XMS memory**.

EMS Memory

Despite the limitations of DOS, some programs can take advantage of memory in a different way by using a "page" method to access

Table 2-1
Storage Capacity of
Floppy Disks

Disk Size	Low Density	High Density
5.25-inch	360KB	1.2MB
3.5-inch	720KB	1.44MB

memory beyond the 1,024KB limit. To use this type of program, not only must your system have extra memory, but the memory must be specially configured as **EMS memory** or expanded memory. This may require special hardware for an 8086 or 286 system.

Disk Drive

Disk drives provide a semipermanent means of storing programs and data. There are two general types: floppy disks and fixed disk drives. There are many variations on size and format, but all store information as magnetic variations, much like music is stored on an audio cassette or video is stored on a VCR tape.

Floppy Disk Drive

Floppy disk drives can be classified according to size and density as shown in Table 2-1. Each type of drive requires a special type of disk. High-density disks cannot be used in a low-density drive. However, it is possible to use a low-density disk in a high-density drive. Caution should be exercised when you use a low-density 5.25-inch disk in a high-density drive, for later you may have occasional trouble reading the disk in a low-density drive. (This caution does not apply to 3.5-inch drives.)

Hard Disk Drive

The most common and most cost-effective mass storage device is a **hard disk drive**, with storage capacities that range from less than 100MB to well over 1,000MB. Most small systems use a drive with an Integrated Drive Electronics (**IDE**) interface. Higher performance drives may use the small computer systems interface (**SCSI**).

Optical Disk Drive

A more recent technology is the laser or **optical disk drive**. These storage devices use platters that are similar to compact disks and are read using lasers. They are available in several formats.

CD-ROM

The compact disk read-only memory, or **CD-ROM**, actually uses the familiar CD format. As the name implies, the disks must be manufactured with the data already encoded since the drive can read from it but not write to it. A typical CD-ROM, increasingly common on the latest "multimedia" systems, stores about 600MB of information.

WORM Drive

Another device, the write-once read-many (**WORM**) optical drive, uses a disk that can be written on only once. Since the data on these disks, once written, cannot be erased, WORM drives are especially useful in situations in which an accurate history of data is essential.

Read-Write Optical Drive

Finally, the most recent innovation in optical drives is the **read-write optical drive**. This type of drive acts much like a hard disk, but is slower and costs more initially. However, the removable nature of the optical disk makes this type of drive advantageous in environments where massive amounts of data must be stored, but only parts of the data need be on-line at any one time.

Tape Drive

While not always included with a standard PC, a **tape drive** is frequently included with at least one computer on a network in order to make backup copies of data. Tape drives come in several standard formats, the most cost-effective being those that use small tape cartridges. Examples are the tape drives based on the QIC-80 standard that store about 250MB per tape and those based on the DAT (digital audio tape) standard that store about 1,300MB (1.3 gigabytes, or 1.3GB) per tape.

Serial and Parallel Ports

Serial ports and **parallel ports** are used to connect devices to the computer. A PC is normally equipped with up to two parallel connections (designated **LPT1:** and **LPT2:**) and two serial connections (designated **COM1:** and **COM2:**). A parallel connection is identified by a 25-pin female connector on the PC and is often used to attach a printer. A serial connection is identified by either a 9-pin or a 25-pin male connector on the PC and is normally used to attach a modem or a mouse to a PC. Some PCs have a separate round connector for plugging in a mouse; this is called a **mouse port**.

Network Interface Card

Normally, a network interface card must be added to a PC in order to connect it to a LAN. This involves setting up the card and plugging it into one of the expansion slots in the PC. The NIC should be set up so that it does not interfere with the operation of any of the other devices that are part of the PC. Once this has been done, the card can be plugged into a network and the necessary software added to the PC.

Choosing a Computer

Overall, hardware capabilities and costs continue to improve by a factor of two about every three years (that is, in about three years you may be able to purchase the same capabilities for about half the price). In practice, the "standard" office computer continues to cost about the same, but is faster and has more capabilities. In most cases, these additional capabilities are dictated by the demands of more sophisticated software and modern graphical user interfaces (GUIs).

Very few computers are being purchased with less than a 386 processor. Part of this trend is driven by the lower cost of more powerful systems, and part can be attributed to the fact that there are already many older systems in place that can be assigned to tasks that do not require the extra capabilities of the newer, faster processors. But the most important factor is the growing popularity of Windows and OS/2 programs, which provide an easy-to-use graphical user interface. These programs make heavier demands on the computer systems and run best on faster 386, 486, or 586 systems.

Typical PC Configurations

The modern PC has a smaller case that takes up less room on the desktop. There are a number of these small footprint systems that would be appropriate for an office LAN. A typical system would have a standard keyboard, a 3.5-inch and/or a 5.25-inch floppy drive, two serial ports, one parallel port, and an IDE drive interface built into the main system circuit board (the motherboard). Other details would vary according to the applications to be run. Here are some examples:

Low-End System for Word Processing

The minimum system configuration might include a 386SX processor running at 20MHz or 25MHz, a 40MB hard disk, and 2MB of system memory. A monochrome VGA display might be acceptable for some situations, but a color display is recommended (and a great deal more interesting to look at).

General-Purpose System

This might be a bit more expensive, but one able to run more demanding software. It might have a 386 or 486SX processor running at 20MHz or 25MHz, an 80MB hard disk, 4MB of system memory, and a color VGA display. With the addition of a mouse, this system would be acceptable for occasional use of Windows.

Windows System

This system would have the power to handle the greater demands that Windows applications place on a system. It would include a 486 processor running at 33MHz, 8MB of system memory, a 100–200MB hard disk, a color super-VGA display, and a mouse. A graphics accelerator and/or local bus video would also enhance performance when using Windows.

Special Considerations for a Network

With the addition of a network interface card (NIC) to allow communication with the LAN server, all of the above configurations are suitable for use on a LAN. However, in many cases the hard disk can be eliminated or reduced to 40–80MB because software can be loaded from the network server. Note that if Windows is to be used, it is not a good idea to eliminate the hard disk altogether. This is because Windows uses a "swap file" to switch contexts between one application and another. The swap file should be on the local hard disk for greater speed and efficiency.

Network Servers

The type of computer system chosen for a network server depends on a variety of factors. These include: the number of users to be served on the network; the types of applications that are running; the network operating system; the version of the operating system; the data storage needs; and the criticality of the applications supported by the server. The exact demands placed on a server would depend on all of these factors. Generally speaking, a server would be able to support fewer users in an environment where there is a need for constant access to very large databases or where graphics-intensive programs are used. In contrast, most word processing applications make relatively small demands on the server.

Since a server supports many users, it is often easier to justify an incremental investment in the server hardware and software. For example, a server running Netware 3.x usually requires at least 4MB of memory. However, the additional cost of procuring 8, 16, or even 32MB of memory can often be justified in terms of overall system performance. Similarly, it is reasonable to consider systems with faster, 32-bit bus architectures such as the IBM PS/2 Micro-Channel or the EISA bus. These systems cost more than PCs that use the standard bus architecture, but they allow the use of faster network interface cards and speedier hard disk controllers, thus boosting overall system performance. Finally, it is usual to consider faster disk drives that use the SCSI standard.

Examples of Server Configurations

A typical network server would use a floor-standing tower case with a large power supply capable of handling the additional memory and larger disk drives likely to be needed. It would be plugged into a UPS to ensure that it could be shut down gracefully in the event of a power outage. It might have a backup tape drive installed in one of the disk drive bays. (If not, a tape drive would be installed in one of the network workstations.) It would not need to have a color monitor. The server might also use the EISA 32-bit bus architecture or the PS/2 MicroChannel. Other aspects of the server would vary depending on the situation. On the next page are some typical configurations.

Low-Cost, Low-Demand Workgroup Server

This might be a 386 ISA system running at 33MHz, with 8MB of memory, a 200–400MB IDE drive, and a 16-bit Ethernet network interface card. This server could be running Netware 2.x or 3.x and would be appropriate for low to medium user-demand situations. In this case, an inexpensive tape drive based on the QIC-80 standard might be installed in a PC for doing backups. This system could serve 5 to 50 users depending on the application mix, but may slow down noticeably with more than 10 to 20 simultaneous users.

Intermediate-to-Large Workgroup Server

The previous low-cost system could be improved in a number of ways. The resulting configuration might include: a 486 EISA system running at 33MHz, 16MB of memory, a 32-bit SCSI-2 controller, a 400–1,000MB SCSI-2 drive, a DAT backup system, and a 32-bit Ethernet network interface card. This system running Netware 3.x could serve 10 to 250 users depending on the application mix, but 30 to 80 users might be typical.

Either of the previous systems might also be a PS/2 or might use a Token Ring NIC instead of Ethernet.

Fault-Tolerant System

In some cases, it is important to prevent data loss or downtime that might result from a server malfunction. The Netware network operating system supports the use of two controllers and drives to store duplicate copies of data. This **disk duplexing** prevents data loss or downtime if one of the drives or controllers goes bad. This provides a significant degree of fault tolerance, since the mass storage system is the most critical part of a server. All versions of Novell Netware provide this capability with an appropriately configured server. A fault-tolerant server might include: a 486 EISA system running at 33MHz, 16MB of memory, two 400–1,000MB SCSI-2 drives, two 32-bit SCSI-2 controllers, and a 32-bit Ethernet network interface card.

RAID

A recent innovation in fault tolerance is the redundant array of inexpensive drives (**RAID**). A RAID system commonly includes 2–5 drives configured in such a way that the loss of any one drive will not cause data loss. Some of these systems are self-contained and can be used with a variety of operating systems. There are several types of RAID devices. The most common are classified as RAID level 1, which is equivalent to disk duplexing; RAID level 3, where one of the disks, called the parity drive, stores error-correcting information; and RAID level 5, a more sophisticated approach where error-correcting information is stored on all drives.

Summary

The IBM-compatible personal computer is the most common type of system connected to a local area network. Almost all PC configurations can be used on a network with the addition of a network interface card and the appropriate software and wiring connections. Before connecting a PC to a network, it is necessary to configure and add the network interface card, and generate the appropriate network shell software.

The most cost-effective PC system for a particular office or organization depends on the anticipated mix of software that will be used on that system. A high-powered PC system is often used as a network server. These systems can be configured to provide network services for 5 to 250 users.

Review Questions

The answers to questions marked by an asterisk are in Appendix B.

* **1.** What are the differences between a CD-ROM drive, a WORM drive, and a hard disk drive?

* **2.** What are some of the factors involved in choosing a computer for a file server?

* **3.** What factors are involved in purchasing a computer that will be connected to a network? What details of its hardware configuration are different from that of one that will not be connected?

4. A business magazine gave the following information about the Intel family of processors:

Processor	MIPS
286	1
386	5
486	20
586	100

What is missing from this table? Are these numbers (for MIPS) consistent with the information in the text?

Exercises

1. Determine the following information about your computer or the typical computer in your organization:

Type of monitor _____.

Type of processor _____. Clock speed _____ MHz.

Amount of system memory installed _____.

Size and capacity of installed drives:

> Size: (3.5", 5.25", hard)   Capacity (KB or MB)

> A: drive _____   _____

> B: drive _____   _____

> C: drive _____   _____

2. Call a computer store or use a mail-order catalog to get prices for systems that are similar to each of the sample workstation and server configurations.

Key Terms

The following terms are introduced in this unit. Be sure that you know what each of them means.

Add-in card

Bits

Byte

CD-ROM

COM1: and COM2:

CPU

Disk duplexing

EMS (expanded) memory

Floppy disk drive

Hard disk drive

High RAM

IDE

Keyboard

Kilobyte

LPT1: and LPT2:

Megabyte

Microprocessor

MIPS

Monitor

Mouse port

Optical disk drive

Parallel port

RAID

Read-write optical drive

SCSI

Serial port

System memory

System unit

Tape drive

Video adapter

WORM drive

XMS (extended) memory

Unit 3 **DOS Concepts**

Most local area networks connect PCs that are running DOS and provide the capability to build on or extend the DOS file structure and functionality. Because of this, it is necessary to have a good understanding of DOS to fully understand local area networks in the PC environment.

Learning Objectives

At the completion of this unit, you should be able to

1. understand the purpose of DOS,
2. know important DOS concepts,
3. use DOS to format disks, copy files, and create directories,
4. create and use DOS batch files.

Purpose of DOS

The **disk operating system (DOS)** controls how the computer communicates with the outside world. In particular, DOS manages the storage of information on your computer's disk drives. DOS provides these services to programs along with an interface that allows you to type DOS commands into the computer. These commands can carry out a number of useful tasks such as preparing disks for use, copying files, or checking how much storage is available on your disk.

DOS Files

A file is the unit of information stored on a disk. Depending on how it was created, a file might contain a program, data, a word processing document, a spreadsheet, or a graphical image.

DOS Prompt

The **DOS prompt** is normally the ">" character and indicates that the system is ready to respond to a DOS command. You can change the displayed character using the **PROMPT** command. Normally,

PROMPT PG is used to display the default drive followed by the ">" character.

◆ DOS File Specification

Each file has a unique "tag" or file specification that may be used to identify it. For example, you may identify a file using the file specification A:\MYFILE.TXT. This file specification has the following parts:

➡ A disk drive designator (A:)

➡ A directory path (\)

➡ A file name (MYFILE)

➡ A file name extension (TXT)

◆ Drive Designator

In the above example, the drive designator A: usually refers to the left or top-most floppy disk drive. It is customary to use letters A: through E: to refer to local drives; A: and B: normally refer to floppy drives and C: normally refers to the internal hard disk.

◆ Directory Path

In this case, the directory path \ indicates that the file is located in the main or **root directory** of the disk (rather than a subdirectory as discussed later). Often the drive and directory path are combined as A:\.

◆ DOS File Names

DOS file names may contain at most eight characters plus an optional extension that is no more than three characters. The file name appears first and the extension, if used, is separated from the name by a period (as in MYFILE.TXT). File names can contain letters, numbers, and some special characters such as underscore (_), dollar sign ($), braces ({}), and parentheses [()]. Spaces cannot be used, so the underscore can be useful for comprehension rather than a space (as in MY_FILE.TXT).

◆ DOS File Extensions

In many cases, the file extension is used to indicate a particular type of file. Some extensions are purely for convenience. For example, the extension .TXT is often used to indicate a "text" file, but has no significance otherwise. Other extensions are widely used by programs when they save data files. For example, .DBF is used for database files compatible with the dBASE standard, and .WK1 is used for Lotus 1-2-3 spreadsheets. The following extensions are DOS conventions and are always used as indicated:

.EXE	An executable (program) file
.COM	A DOS image file (also executable)
.BAT	A DOS batch file (with executable DOS commands)
.SYS	A file that contains system information or a hardware driver

The Novell Netware network operating system has its own set of conventions for file extensions. Here are some examples of file extensions used with version 3.x servers:

.NLM   A Netware Loadable Module that provides an enhancement to Netware

.LAN   Driver interface software for a network interface card

.DSK   Driver interface software for a type of disk drive

File Specification Examples

A complete file specification includes the drive designator and directory path and is typed without spaces between the different parts.

`A:\X`   Shortest possible file name (1 character)

`A:\THISFILE.EXT`   Longest possible file name (8 plus 3 characters)

`a:\MYFILE.txt`   Case does not make a difference

Default Drive and Directory Path

DOS keeps track of a "default" or current drive and directory path. If you type a file designator without one of these parts, DOS assumes the default value. For example, `A:THISFILE.TXT` does not include the directory path and so DOS would use the current default path for drive A:. Similarly, DOS would assume the current drive designator for `\THISFILE.TXT`.

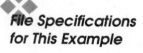

Directory Structures

When dealing with large drives that can store hundreds or even thousands of files, it is necessary for practical purposes to organize the files into directories. A **directory** can be thought of as a compartment that can contain files or other directories. The term **subdirectory** is used when a directory is thought of as being contained in another directory.

Figure 3-1 depicts a drive that has been divided into directories. The main or root directory (\) has two subdirectories, DOS and BAT. The DOS subdirectory contains files and a subdirectory called UTIL.

File Specifications for This Example

This directory structure implies the following file specifications:

`C:\COMMAND.COM`   In the root directory

`C:\BAT\WP.BAT`   In the BAT subdirectory

`C:\DOS\FORMAT.COM`   In the DOS subdirectory

`C:\DOS\UTIL\BAC.COM`   In the UTIL subdirectory of the DOS directory

The same directory structure can be represented using a "family tree" diagram as shown in Figure 3-2. This is a little less precise in representing all of the features of the directory structure, but it is more commonly used and some find it easier to understand.

Figure 3-1
Example of a Hard Disk Directory Structure

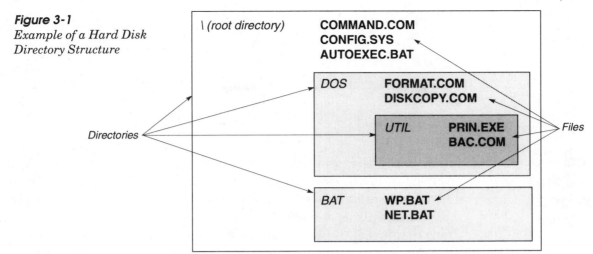

Figure 3-2
Hard Disk Directory Structure Shown in a Tree Diagram

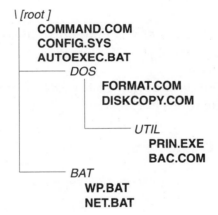

DOS Wild Cards

The symbols * and ? are used as "wild cards" and have special meanings when used in a DOS file specification.

The asterisk * stands for an arbitrary string of characters of any length. Thus, *.COM would include any file name with an extension of .COM and can be used in a DOS command to refer to any and all such files. For example, typing the DOS command

    DIR *.COM

would list all files with an extension of .COM. These would include files with names like COMMAND.COM and PRINT.COM. The DOS command

    ERASE *.TXT

would erase all files with an extension of .TXT. (*Be careful with this one.*)

The question mark **?** stands for an arbitrary single character. For example,

```
DIR ????T.COM
```

would list files like **PRINT.COM** and **TTTTT.COM** but not **ART.COM** or **MARTY.COM**.

Guided Tour—Using Drives and Directories

When using the computer, remember that DOS keeps track of a **current drive** or **default drive** and directory. The default drive is normally displayed as part of the DOS prompt. It can be changed by typing a new drive designation. The current directory **path** is sometimes displayed as part of the DOS prompt, but can always be displayed by typing **CD** or **CHDIR** at the DOS prompt. **CD** or **CHDIR** when followed by a path will cause DOS to change the current directory to the one specified.

Prompt

Use the **PROMPT PG** command to have DOS display the current directory as part of the DOS prompt.

Changing the Default Drive

Type a drive designation at the DOS prompt to change the default drive designation. For example:

A:	Change to the A: drive
C:	Change to the C: drive

Listing the Files in a Directory

Use **DIR** (display directory) to see a list of files and directories in the current or designated directory:

DIR	List all files in the current directory
**DIR **	List all files in the root directory of the current drive
DIR C:\DOS*.*	List all files in the DOS directory on the C: drive

Changing the Default Directory Path

Use **CD** (change directory) to change from the current directory to a new default directory on the default or designated drive. The special form **CD ..** is used to change to the **parent directory**, that is, the directory that contains the current one.

**CD **	Change to the root on the current drive
CD DOS	Change to the DOS subdirectory of current directory
CD UTIL	Change to the UTIL subdirectory of current directory
CD BAT	Change to the BAT subdirectory of current directory
CD \BAT	Change to the BAT subdirectory of the root directory
CD ..	Go up one level to the parent directory of the current directory

Creating a New Directory

Use MD (make directory) to create new directories.

MD BAT	Make a BAT subdirectory of the current directory
MD C:DOS	Make a DOS subdirectory of the current directory of the C: drive
MD C:\DOS\UTIL	Make a UTIL subdirectory of the DOS directory on the C: drive

Using the COPY Command

The DOS COPY command can be used to copy one or more files to another disk or directory. For example:

COPY *.* A:	Copy all files from the current directory on the current drive to current directory on the A: drive
COPY *.* UTIL	Copy all files from the current directory to the UTIL subdirectory, if there is one
COPY C:\BAT*.BAT A:	Copy all batch files (those ending with .BAT) from the BAT subdirectory of the C: drive to current directory on the A: drive

Formatting a Disk

A new disk must be prepared (formatted) before you can use it. Unless it was formatted at the factory, it must be prepared using the DOS FORMAT command before you use it for the first time. The FORMAT command has several options including the following:

FORMAT A:	Format a disk in drive A: (high-density drive formats at high density, low-density drive formats at low density)
FORMAT A: /n:9/t:80	Format a 720KB disk in a high-density 3.5" drive
FORMAT A: /f:720	Format a 720KB disk in a high-density 3.5" drive; this is the newer syntax used with DOS 5 and is preferable to the /n:9/t:80 form

Note *Formatting a disk destroys all data on the disk. It is especially important not to accidentally format a hard disk drive (drive C: or above). Although DOS 5 and above sometimes allows you to UNFORMAT a floppy disk, it is not a good idea to rely on this feature.*

The DOS Search Path

DOS uses the PATH specification to keep track of places to look for program or command files. These are files that end with the extension .EXE, .COM, or .BAT.

For example, you may wish to place all batch files into the BAT directory on the C: drive and all DOS command files into the DOS directory on the C:\ drive. The following PATH command would tell DOS to search these directories to find command or batch files to execute. Once the search path has been established, you can type a command such as **FORMAT A:** or the name of a batch file and DOS will find the appropriate file if it is in the current directory or in a directory specified in the PATH statement.

PATH = C:\DOS;C:\BAT   Tells DOS to look in the DOS and BAT directories for programs, command procedures, or batch files

The DOS Environment

The DOS environment can be customized in a number of ways. For example, the DOS prompt can be set up to show the current drive and directory path using the PROMPT command as shown in the Guided Tour. System variables can also be set up using commands of the form:

TEMP = C:\WINDOWS\TEMP

In this case, the value of **TEMP** tells programs where to locate temporary work files.

You can determine environment parameters by typing the command **SET** at the DOS prompt.

The CONFIG.SYS File

CONFIG.SYS is a file used to customize DOS and to add support for unique hardware or custom software that might be used in your computer. When the computer starts, it checks the CONFIG.SYS file and carries out the commands in it.

The exact statements you will need to place in your CONFIG.SYS file will vary from one situation to another, but a typical CONFIG.SYS file might contain lines of the form:

```
FILES = 50
BUFFERS = 10
DEVICE = C:\DOS\HIMEM.SYS    Extended memory manager
DEVICE = C:\ANSI.SYS         Standard screen interface
DEVICE = C:\MSMOUSE.SYS      Driver for mouse
```

DOS Batch Files

A DOS **batch file** provides a handy way to automate one or more DOS tasks. For example, you can use the batch file shown in Figure 3-3, called FORMLO.BAT, to format low-density 3.5" disks in a high-density drive. Once the file has been created, execute the commands by typing **FORMLO A:** or **FORMLO B:** at the DOS prompt. The parameter A: or B: is passed to the batch file as the variable %1.

Figure 3-3
FORMLO.BAT

```
ECHO OFF
CLS
ECHO This will format a LOW density disk.
PAUSE
FORMAT  %1  /N:9/T:80
```

Creating a Batch File

Use a text editor, or the following special form of the COPY command, to create a batch file. In this case, you are instructing the computer to copy characters from the keyboard console (CON:) directly into a DOS file.

COPY CON: FORMLO.BAT	Will begin to store keystrokes for the file FORMLO.BAT
<file contents>	Type line after line of text to include in the file
^Z	Finish by typing Ctrl-Z and press Enter.

Branching in a Batch File

DOS permits a crude form of branching using an IF statement within a batch file. Here is an example that provides a modification of the FORMLO.BAT procedure given above:

IF %1==A: GOTO forma	Branch if FORMLO A: was typed
IF %1==B: GOTO formb	Branch if FORMLO B: was typed
GOTO end	
:forma	
FORMAT A: /n:9 /T:80	Format for drive A:
GOTO end	
:formb	
FORMAT B: /4	Format for drive B:
:end	

AUTOEXEC.BAT

The **AUTOEXEC.BAT** file (discussed in Unit 4) plays a special role in setting up a PC. When a PC starts, DOS automatically carries out the commands in this file. DOS provides a number of tools for using PC drives and files, and for organizing files into directories.

Summary

A well-thought-out directory structure can make it easy to find a file or program on your drive. Later, in Unit 13, we will see that a well-organized directory structure is especially important when dealing with a network drive that may contain thousands of files. DOS batch files can be used to automate tasks by carrying out a group of DOS commands at once. CONFIG.SYS and AUTOEXEC.BAT play a special role in setting up the PC environment.

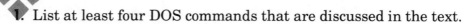

Review Questions

1. List at least four DOS commands that are discussed in the text.

* 2. What does the FORMAT command do? Would you ever want to format the C: drive on your computer?

Exercises

1. Figures 3-1 and 3-2 illustrate a directory structure. Represent the same structure in terms of file folders.

2. The example for branching in a batch procedure does not do anything if you type FORMLO A: because the IF comparison is case-sensitive. Modify the procedure to allow for both uppercase and lowercase parameters.

3. The example MD C:\DOS\UTIL appears in the Guided Tour. In that context, what would have happened if MD UTIL were typed instead?

Key Terms

AUTOEXEC.BAT

Batch file

CONFIG.SYS

Current drive

Default drive

Directory

Disk operating system (DOS)

DOS prompt

Parent directory

Path

PROMPT

Root directory

Subdirectory

Unit 4 Setting Up a PC to Operate on a Network

Most DOS PCs can be connected to a network by adding a network interface card (NIC) and the appropriate software to allow communication with the LAN server. This section outlines the process that is used to prepare a PC for connection to an existing LAN.

Learning Objectives

At the completion of this unit, you should be able to

1. outline the steps needed to prepare a computer to operate on a network,
2. write an AUTOEXEC.BAT file for your computer,
3. automate the process of logging into a network,
4. understand the options for setting up a network workstation.

Prepare the PC

If you are installing a new PC, it must first be prepared properly to run DOS (the disk operating system) as well as other software such as Windows, if appropriate. Normally, the PC should already have at least 1MB of memory. If this is not the case, you may wish to add memory because some of it will be used by the network software. (The network shell program uses about 55KB of memory over and above that required for your usual DOS software.)

Prepare Workstation Files

The workstation shell programs extend DOS to enable a PC to function properly in a network environment. The details of setting up a workstation can depend on factors such as the type of network adapter card, the settings used on the card, the operating environment, and the version of Netware.

Workstation files IPX.COM and NETX.COM are commonly used with Netware 2 and 3 servers. The IPX.COM file is hardware-specific and must be set up to operate with the NIC. This is done using the WSGEN Netware utility program.

Configure and Install the Adapter Card

Once the NIC settings have been determined, the adapter card will need to be set up properly to operate in the workstation. This may mean relocating "jumpers" (little devices that connect pins together on the expansion board) to set the parameters that are used to communicate between the computer and the network board. The newer MicroChannel or EISA boards use a setup program instead of jumpers.

Three parameters must be set in configuring the board and the software: **interrupt level**, I/O address, and high memory address. Each of these must be set to be consistent with the settings used when the IPX file (or other workstation file) was set up, and should not conflict with the settings used by other boards or devices in the computer. If you go through this process and the factory default settings do not work, you will need to identify the conflict and reconfigure the workstation files to use values that do not conflict with the hardware. You may also need to reset the jumpers on the NIC.

Commonly Used Interrupts

Table 4-1 shows the traditional uses for the most common interrupts in an AT-compatible computer. This information can be useful if you are trying to eliminate a hardware conflict. For example, if your computer has only one parallel port (LPT1:), you can normally use interrupt 5 for the network board.

Table 4-1
Common Interrupt Uses

Device	Interrupt	I/O Address
LPT1:	IRQ 7	378-37F or 3BC-3BE*
LPT2:	IRQ 5	278-27F or 378-37A*
LPT3:*	none	278-27A*
COM1:	IRQ 4	3F8-3FF
COM2:	IRQ 3	2F8-2FF
Floppy disk drive	IRQ 6	1F0-1F8 / 3F0-3F7
Hard disk drive	IRQ 14	1F0-1F8 / 3F0-3F7

* Used only when there are three LPT ports

Connect the Computer to the Network

After the above steps are performed, the computer is ready to connect to the network. However, there are still some things that might need to be done to automate the process of loading the software necessary to operate on the network. These are discussed below.

◆◆
**Automating
the Startup Process
with** AUTOEXEC.BAT

When a PC starts, DOS automatically carries out the commands contained in the AUTOEXEC.BAT file. This is where you would place commands to initialize the Netware shell.

◆◆
**A Typical
AUTOEXEC.BAT **File

A typical network AUTOEXEC.BAT file might contain statements of the form:

```
PROMPT $P$G
PATH = C:\;C:\DOS;C:\WINDOWS
C:\MOUSE
C:\WINDOWS\SMARTDRV
IPX
NETX
F:
LOGIN
```

This includes some DOS commands such as PROMPT and PATH that were mentioned in Unit 3 and a command MOUSE to load a mouse "driver" that enables the computer to communicate with a mouse.

The last four commands load the Netware shell program and begin the login process. As an alternative, these commands can be placed in another batch file called, say, **STARTNET.BAT**. In this case the user will not be connected to the network until the STARTNET command is typed at the DOS prompt. (The Netware 4 workstation installation program, discussed below, automates this process.)

◆◆
**Booting Remotely
from a Diskless
Workstation**

Using a specially equipped network card, it is possible to boot a PC that has no disk drives. In this case, the DOS system along with the workstation program must be provided in a special format on the server. The network administrator sets this up by running a program called DOSGEN to create a special boot file on the server.

◆◆
**Netware ODI
Workstation
Programs**

The Open Data-Link Interface (**ODI**) was introduced with Netware 3 and provides a more flexible way to set up a network workstation. ODI separates the functionality of IPX into a part that is hardware-specific and parts that are not. (The latter are implemented as **LSL.COM** and **IPXODI.COM**.) The hardware-specific portion is configured through settings in the file **NET.CFG**.

ODI Configuration

For example, a DOS workstation in a Netware 3 environment using a 3Com 3C503 network adapter might use the following:

AUTOEXEC.BAT

```
PROMPT $P$G
PATH = C:\;C:\DOS;C:\WINDOWS
C:\MOUSE
C:\WINDOWS\SMARTDRV
LSL
3C503
IPXODI
NETX
F:
LOGIN
```

NET.CFG

```
LINK DRIVER 3C503
INT 3
PORT 300
```

Similarly, a configuration using a Netware NE2000 NIC might use the same AUTOEXEC.BAT file with the line **3C503** replaced by **NE2000**, and a NET:CFG file of the form:

NET.CFG

```
LINK DRIVER NE2000
INT 4
PORT 320
MEM D000
```

DOS and Memory Management

The Netware workstation shell programs require a significant amount of RAM. This makes memory management especially important in a network environment.

DOS 5 and DOS 6, when installed on a 386 or higher system, provide the capability to use memory beyond the usual 640KB DOS limit. This capability is implemented using the device drivers HIMEM.SYS and EMM386.EXE.

With DOS 5, the setup and use of these drivers are relatively complex. However, DOS 6 provides a program called MEMMAKER that automates the setup of these drivers and optimizes the use of memory.

Netware and Windows

Almost all of the newer DOS systems use Windows as a primary user interface. Windows 3.1 is network-aware and integrates well with Netware, provided a few basic rules are followed. (The most important are: login to the network before starting Windows, and logout after ending Windows.)

Windows for Workgroups

Windows for Workgroups (WFW) is a version of Windows that provides integrated networking capabilities. It is a peer-to-peer system, whereby all users can provide and access resources such as hard disks and printers. The package also provides E-mail and scheduling and allows connection to a Novell file server.

Netware DOS Requester

The **Netware DOS Requester**, introduced with Netware 4, replaces the NETX shell and provides both additional features and the tighter security required by Netware 4. The requester uses virtual loadable modules (**VLMs**) as a flexible way to provide functionality. The VLMs are more tightly integrated with DOS and include better support for the use of Windows. In addition, the VLM programs load into extended memory, thereby freeing additional DOS memory.

The DOS requester uses an installation program to automate the process of setting up a PC as a network workstation. This program copies the necessary files to the PC, makes changes to CONFIG.SYS and AUTOEXEC.BAT, and creates a startup file called STARTNET.BAT.

Summary

Setting up a PC to operate on a network involves the installation of hardware and software to extend the capabilities of DOS. The special batch file AUTOEXEC.BAT executes automatically when a computer is started. This file can be modified to include the Netware startup commands. Network startup commands can also be placed in the batch file STARTNET.

Review Questions

* 1. What are the commands that are necessary to connect a computer to a Novell network?

2. What are the roles of AUTOEXEC.BAT and NET.CFG in setting up a PC to operate on a network?

* **3.** Outline *all* of the steps required to get a computer to operate on a network. Assume that you can get copies of the IPX and NETX files from your network administrator.

Exercises

1. Write a batch file called CONNECT.BAT to automate the process of connecting to a network in the event that the necessary commands are not in the AUTOEXEC.BAT file.

2. Run the Novell WSGEN utility to create an IPX file for a particular network interface card.

Key Terms

Interrupt level

IPXODI.COM

LSL.COM

NET.CFG

Netware DOS Requester

ODI

STARTNET.BAT

VLM

Unit 5 **LAN Standards**

Standards are important in any field of endeavor, but they are even more important for networks if we need to link diverse computers running different operating systems. In this case, networks can provide functional linkages only if there is a standard way for the computers to communicate. Standards also provide a uniform way to define these linkages.

Learning Objectives

At the completion of this unit, you should be able to

1. understand the role that standards play in networking,

2. recognize the primary standards and what they provide,

3. appreciate the diversity of network functions as specified in the OSI model.

The Ways that Standards Are Set

There are two ways in which standards are defined and accepted. Large corporations, like IBM and Microsoft, can set standards arbitrarily. These are likely to be accepted because of the large base of users that will adopt the standard. These standards are set after the fact and, hence, are known as de facto standards. Other standards are set by industry committees that have wide support from participating corporations. These standards are sometimes set before products using them are widely available.

OSI (Open Systems Interconnection)

Open Systems Interconnection (**OSI**) is a framework for an evolving set of products that facilitate multivendor connectivity. OSI provides a set of parameters and specifications that allow different products from competing vendors to communicate.

OSI as a Way to Understand Network Protocols

The OSI model not only provides a collection of networking standards, but also furnishes a means of viewing the inner workings of a network. OSI can help us understand the complex variety of protocols and applications that are part of the study of network technology. Because the OSI model is meant to include complex networks that may link thousands of sites at widely dispersed locations, some of the functions are not required for a local area network.

The OSI Seven-Layer Architecture

The OSI model divides network hardware and software into seven distinct parts, as shown in Figure 5-1. Each has a standard that defines functionality and means of communication with other layers in the model. Here is a brief description, starting with the highest layer (layer 7).

7. **Application layer**. This is the layer that the user or the user's application sees. This might include services like electronic mail or the ability to copy a file from one place to another across the network.

6. **Presentation layer**. This controls how information is represented and special characters are displayed, or interpreted, in order to create a standard application interface. Data encryption, or compression and decompression, would happen at this layer.

5. **Session layer**. The session layer provides the controls that enable two network processes or applications to communicate across a network. The processes on this layer establish, manage, and terminate virtual connections or sessions on the network. NETBIOS (discussed below) is a session layer protocol and gateways operate on all layers up to this level.

Figure 5-1
OSI Model

| Application |
| Presentation |

Presenting the Information to the User

| Session |
| Transport |

Providing a Connection and Moving Information across the Network

| Network |
| Data Link |

Moving Bits Around

| Physical |

4. **Transport layer**. This layer is concerned with error-free communication between end-points in a session. This layer handles error recovery and controls the flow of information between the two ends of the virtual connection.

3. **Network layer**. This layer is responsible both for establishing, maintaining, and terminating connections and for the routing and switching required to get messages to the right place. Conceptually, this layer separates the logical processes and protocols of the upper layers from the technical details of how the systems are physically connected.

2. **Data link layer**. This layer provides for reliable transfer of blocks of data or "frames" across a physical link (point-to-point connectivity). It also handles errors and flow control at the frame level.

1. **Physical layer**. This layer provides standards for the transmission of bits across the physical link. This includes standards for the transmission medium (wire, fiber, and so on) and the electrical characteristics of the signal. It also handles the assignment and use of physical addresses of each network node, while providing methods of establishing, maintaining, and deactivating the physical link.

Lower Layer Network Standards

Lower layer standards apply to network hardware components and ways in which the signals are encoded on the wire or other medium. These standards operate at the physical and data link layers of the OSI model and include network technologies such as Ethernet, Token Ring, and 10Base-T (all to be covered). They help ensure that a specific type of hardware from one vendor can communicate with the same type of hardware from another vendor.

The 802.x Standards

International standards for Ethernet and Token Ring are part of a larger group of standards published by the American National Standards Institute (ANSI) and a European committee called CCIT. These include standards for Ethernet (802.3) and for Token Ring (802.5) and are collectively referred to as the **802.x standards**. These include hardware-specific issues (wire and connection specifications) as well as standards for signal and frame characteristics.

Packets

When devices communicate on a network, they send information a "chunk" at a time. This chunk, called a **packet**, must have a specific format to adhere to the standard. For example, the 802.3 Ethernet standard packet has an introductory "preamble" followed by five parts that provide a destination address, source address, length, data, and error check sum. Each 802.3 Ethernet packet must have these segments in a specific order, starting with the destination address, and of a specific length as shown in Figure 5-2.

Figure 5-2
Ethernet Packet

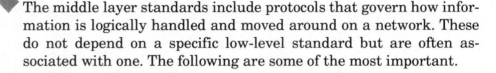

	6 Bytes	6 Bytes	2 Bytes	From 46 to 1500 Bytes	4 Bytes
	Destination	Source	Length	Data	CRC-32

10Base-T

10Base-T is a recent standard for a version of Ethernet that uses twisted pair wiring and a different method of encoding the signal on the wire (but the same packet format). Because the higher level protocols at the data link layer are similar to 802.3 Ethernet, the 10Base-T standard differs from 802.3 primarily in the lowest (physical) layer specification.

Middle Layer Network Standards

The middle layer standards include protocols that govern how information is logically handled and moved around on a network. These do not depend on a specific low-level standard but are often associated with one. The following are some of the most important.

XNS/IPX

XNS (or Xerox Network Services) is normally associated with the original version of Ethernet. **IPX** (or Internet Packet eXchange) refers to a variant that is used on Novell networks.

NETBIOS

NETwork Basic Input/Output System (**NETBIOS**) is a software system developed by IBM and Sytek for the original IBM PC network. It has since become popular as a high-level session layer interface for PC networks. Some networking schemes use it directly (IBM and Lantastic), while others (Novell, Banyan, and the like) provide indirect support through emulation.

TCP/IP

Transmission Control Protocol/Internet Protocol (**TCP/IP**) is a network protocol suite commonly used to link government research and education networks. TCP/IP is supported by virtually all computer systems manufacturers. The standard was developed by the Department of Defense (DOD), which has promoted adherence by requiring it in any systems that it purchases as well as by instituting a testing and certification program. As a result, TCP/IP is widely used and supported and is a viable way to interconnect a variety of hardware. TCP/IP transport protocols are supported in versions 3.11 and later of Netware.

Upper Layer Network Standards

Upper layer standards provide services such as mail services or distributed file systems. These are often associated with specific middle layer protocols.

Figure 5-3
OSI Model and TCP/IP

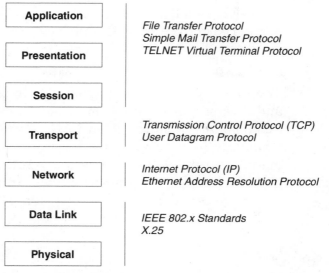

File Transfer Protocol
Simple Mail Transfer Protocol
TELNET Virtual Terminal Protocol

Transmission Control Protocol (TCP)
User Datagram Protocol

Internet Protocol (IP)
Ethernet Address Resolution Protocol

IEEE 802.x Standards
X.25

(TCP/IP Predates the OSI Model)

FTP, SMTP, and TELNET

There are three upper-layer standards that are normally part of the standard TCP/IP suite, as illustrated in Figure 5-3: File Transfer Protocol (**FTP**) is a utility for copying files across a TCP/IP network, Simple Mail Transfer Protocol (**SMTP**) is a standard mail service available on TCP/IP networks, and **TELNET** is a terminal emulation service that can provide remote access to a computer attached to a TCP/IP network.

Distributed File Systems

A distributed file system provides a set of standards for sharing files on a network. Most LAN operating systems that operate with PCs provide a distributed file system that is similar to the DOS file system. Netware provides a file system that looks to the user like the file system on the local system, be it DOS, UNIX, OS/2, or Macintosh.

NFS

The Network File System (**NFS**) is a widely used, distributed file system standard, especially in the UNIX environment. It was developed as an extension to the UNIX operating system in 1984 by Sun Microsystems and was placed in the public domain so that other companies could develop compatible products. More than one hundred companies and universities have licensed NFS, and it has become a standard for UNIX workstations.

Netware and Standards

Novell Netware is a proprietary system that nevertheless has become a standard because of its wide use. In addition, Netware supports many of the standards mentioned here such as TCP/IP, which is available as part of Netware 3.11 and later. Another Novell product, Lan Workplace, provides client support for FTP, SMTP, and

TELNET. Finally, NFS server support is available as an optional module with Netware 3.11 and above.

Summary

The OSI model provides a good way to understand the complexity and diversity of functions on a network, although not all of these functions are required for a LAN. The 802.x and other hardware standards help ensure that hardware components from different manufacturers will interoperate on the same network. Novell Netware, as well as protocol standards, operate in the middle-to-upper layers of the OSI model and, hence, can be mixed and matched with different hardware.

Review Questions

* 1. The OSI standards can be grouped into three categories as shown in Figure 5-1. Where do the 802.x standards and the Novell IPX standards fit into this picture?

* 2. How does 10Base-T differ from standard Ethernet?

Exercises

1. Use the information in the text to determine the length of the shortest and longest possible standard Ethernet packet.

2. Determine whether TCP/IP or OSI protocols are in use on your network or a network you are familiar with. If so, what are they used for?

Key Terms

10Base-T

802.x standards

Application layer

Data link layer

FTP

IPX

NETBIOS

Network layer

NFS

OSI

Packet

Physical layer

Presentation layer

Session layer

SMTP

TCP/IP

TELNET

Transport layer

XNS

Unit 6 Laying Out a LAN

The physical layout or arrangement of LAN wiring can be an important element of the planning process, depending on the specific type of LAN adapter chosen for use in the workstations and the network file server. This unit will discuss some details that are associated with wiring types and arrangements, providing background for the specific LAN technologies to be discussed next.

Learning Objectives

At the completion of this unit, you should be able to

1. appreciate the major wiring types and layouts,
2. understand the differences in grades of twisted pair wires,
3. identify the most common standard wiring schemes.

Wiring Arrangement (Topology)

There are several ways that the wires and connections can be arranged. These include **bus**, **star**, ring, and star-wired ring. The majority of wiring schemes use either a bus or a star arrangement. The bus **topology** (physical layout) provides a common circuit (bus) that runs through a building; each station is connected to it. The star topology employs one or more central distribution points where stations are connected to a common hub, as shown in Figure 6-1.

Wire Types

A variety of types of wire can be used for a LAN. These include twisted pair, shielded twisted pair, coaxial cable (also called coax), and fiber optics. Twisted pair is similar in appearance to standard telephone wiring. Shielded twisted pair wire is usually made of heavier 22-gauge wire and has a foil shield around each pair. **Coaxial cable** comes in several varieties but is similar in construction to standard cable TV wire. Fiber optics cable also comes in several varieties, but a standard "multimode" type is normally used for local area and wide area network applications. Each has its characteristic

Figure 6-1
Bus and Star Topology

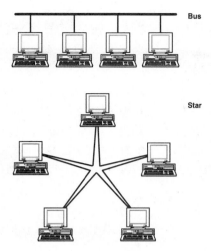

set of costs and capabilities. Generally speaking, the less sophisticated wiring, such as twisted pair or telephone wire, is often used for
short-distance connections within a LAN, while a higher-quality medium such as fiber optics is often used for long-distance connections
between buildings or to interconnect LANs at different sites.

Standard Wiring Schemes

Several standard wiring schemes can be used to wire a building or
site. The IBM Cabling System uses shielded and unshielded twisted
pair and is optimized for Token Ring and other high-speed twisted
pair applications. Digital's DECconnect system uses coaxial cable
and offers several alternatives for a wide range of connectivity options. The AT&T Premises Distribution System (PDS) uses a combination of unshielded twisted pair cable and fiber optics.

The type of wiring scheme you choose depends, in part, on your
hardware vendor and the type of network you use. Whether or not
you choose a standard wiring scheme, some wiring requirements
will be determined by the type of LAN adapter used in your network.
Ethernet, thin Ethernet, and most Arcnet adapter cards usually
require specific types of coaxial cable. Token Ring 16 adapters usually require a specific type of high-quality **shielded twisted pair**.

Twisted Pair

Twisted pair is the most popular type of wiring. It is inexpensive, it
is easy to work with, and it is often already in place. Since it can cost
between $60 and $200 to provide or move each LAN connection, the
use of existing twisted pair wiring can sometimes represent a con-
siderable savings. However, there are many different types of
twisted pair wires, and some may not be appropriate for high-speed
data applications. If in doubt, have the wiring tested to ensure that
it is capable of carrying data.

Table 6-1
Electrical Characteristics of
Twisted Pair Wiring

Description	Electrical Characteristics	Typical Uses
Level 1 Quad Cable	24–26 AWG (not twisted)	Analog voice
Level 2 NTI, RS-232	22–24 AWG, 100±20 Ω impedance 10dB/1,000 ft. attenuation @ 1MHz	Digital voice AppleTalk
Level 3—ISDN IBM Type 3 AT&T PDS	22–24 AWG, 100±10 Ω impedance 8dB/1,000 ft. attenuation @ 1MHz 27.4dB/1,000 ft. @ 10MHz	Digital voice 10Base-T Token Ring 4
Level 4 IBM Types 1, 2	22 AWG, 150±10 Ω impedance 6.4dB/1,000 ft. attenuation @ 4MHz 12.2dB/1,000 ft. @ 16MHz	Token Ring 16

Table 6-1 indicates some of the different qualities of twisted pair wiring. ("Ohms" [Ω] is a measure of electrical resistance, and "dB" or deciBells a measure of the signal loss.)

Fiber Optics and FDDI

Fiber optics is becoming a more popular medium for providing a high-bandwidth data path, usually linking larger LANs or multi-user systems. Recent advances have made it easier to splice and connect fiber optic strands, thereby making the technology more accessible for smaller installations.

Fiber optic products are available to support a number of protocols, including Ethernet and Token Ring. **FDDI** is an emerging standard for transmission along fiber at a rate of 100Mbps (megabits per second). The technology today is at the point where the network manager should consider the incorporation of fiber optic carriers whenever new cable is run between major sites.

Plenum Cable

Most wiring uses a polyvinyl-chloride (PVC) plastic insulator. This type of wire gives off toxic fumes when caught in a fire. Therefore, most building codes require that this type of wire be run through conduits. If your installation does not permit the use of conduits, specially constructed **plenum** wire must be used. This type of wire uses a teflon insulator that does not give off toxic fumes when it burns.

Wiring Costs

Wiring costs for a LAN can vary from almost nothing, if the wire is already installed, to several hundred dollars each for fiber optics connections. Generally speaking, standard 10Base-T twisted pair is the cheapest to install and provides the most flexibility. Plenum wire is usually significantly more expensive than the same type of PVC wire. Nevertheless, the labor cost is usually the most significant and can bring total installation costs for twisted pair to approximately $60–$180 per connection. Higher costs would apply to coaxial and shielded twisted pair, while fiber optics is usually the most expensive because of the higher costs of terminating the fiber. However, fiber optics can be used for long distances, provides the highest data-carrying capacity, and is electrically neutral—the clear choice for backbone networks and high-speed interconnects between buildings.

If you need to rewire a building or plan the wiring for a new building, it is a wise policy to provide additional connections to each station. This is because the marginal cost of providing an additional connection is small in comparison to the cost of providing the first one.

Summary

In some cases, existing twisted pair wiring can be certified for use with networks. Otherwise, the type of wiring provided to each station might depend on the computer hardware you are using. In any case, it is wise to consider providing additional connections to each station.

Review Questions

* 1. What kind of wire is the lowest cost to install for relatively short runs?

* 2. What standard wiring schemes are mentioned in the text and which major computer companies do they represent?

* 3. What situations are appropriate for fiber optics?

* 4. What is plenum wire and when should it be used? Why not use it all of the time?

Exercises

1. Determine the following information for your LAN or one you are familiar with:

   Type of network adapter cards: _____.
   Manufacturer: _____.
   Type of wire used for the network: _____.
   Wiring scheme used (if any): _____.

2. Obtain a sample of twisted pair wire and Token Ring shielded twisted pair.

3. Call a supply house or consult a catalog to determine the price per foot of the following types of wire in both PVC and plenum versions:

   a. Standard AT&T telephone wire
   b. 10Base-T approved twisted pair
   c. IBM Type 1 shielded twisted pair
   d. Thin Ethernet

Key Terms   Bus

Coaxial cable

FDDI

Fiber optics

Plenum

Shielded twisted pair

Star

Topology

Twisted pair

Unit 7 **Ethernet**

Ethernet was the first widely used networking scheme. The original specification was developed at the Xerox Palo Alto Research Center (PARC) in 1976. It was initially used to interconnect large computers and was soon adopted by Digital Equipment Corporation (DEC) and other vendors. There are two slightly different versions of Ethernet. The first is referred to as Ethernet v2.0 (the Xerox-Intel-DEC standard) and the other as IEEE 802.3. The international standard 802.3 is nearly identical to Ethernet v2.0. However, the two standards are not completely compatible, so it is important to be aware of the difference.

Note *In the following discussion, the term "Ethernet" will refer to the 802.3 standard unless "Ethernet v2.0" is specifically mentioned.*

Learning Objectives

At the completion of this unit, you should be able to

1. describe the major components of an Ethernet,
2. list its strengths and weaknesses,
3. appreciate how the Ethernet protocol works,
4. understand the acronym CSMA/CD.

Wiring and Components

Ethernet uses an adapter card and a transmitter to communicate over a thick (orange) coaxial cable. A variant of the 802.3 standard that runs on thinner coaxial cable is normally used on PCs. (This variant is often called **thin Ethernet** or **cheapernet**.) This type of Ethernet has the transceiver built into the adapter card that goes into the PC. This makes installation of thin Ethernet simple and straightforward: Insert the adapter card into the PC and run a wire from one PC to the next. Each adapter card is connected using a "T"

Figure 7-1
Typical Ethernet Layout

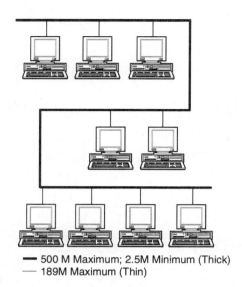

— 500 M Maximum; 2.5M Minimum (Thick)
— 189M Maximum (Thin)

connector that allows the PC to tap into the line without disturbing the circuit. A typical Ethernet configuration is shown in Figure 7-1.

The CSMA/CD Protocol

Ethernet pioneered the protocol called Carrier Sense Multiple Access with Collision Detection (CSMA/CD). With CSMA, each station listens to the line for messages addressed to it. All stations hear all messages, but they only act on ones addressed to them. If a station has a message to transmit, it waits until the line is not busy and then attempts to broadcast its message. A **collision** occurs when two stations start to transmit at the same time. In this case, each detects the "collision", sends out a collision warning signal, and then waits a random length of time (usually milliseconds) before listening again for a clear line to transmit.

Strengths

Ethernet offers a number of advantages as a networking option. It is a widely used system that has become an industry standard. Many third-party vendors produce Ethernet components that run a large base of standard software such as TCP/IP. Ethernet is also relatively cost-effective. Because of its popularity, the cost of Ethernet components has been steadily decreasing while performance has improved. Ethernet also provides a relatively high data transfer rate of 10Mbps, which is more than adequate for most needs.

Weaknesses

Ethernet has a few drawbacks. Standard Ethernet requires special coaxial cable that can be relatively difficult and expensive to install. Ethernet sometimes suffers degradation when the system gets busy. The CSMA/CD protocol performance deteriorates rapidly at 60 to 80 percent of the theoretical limit. Ethernet problems can be relatively difficult to troubleshoot, and it is even possible for a bad station (nicknamed a **jabber**) to jam the circuit and incapacitate the entire network.

Ethernet Design Parameters

An Ethernet **segment** consists of an electrically continuous section of cable. Ethernet segments can be joined, using repeaters or other electronic devices that amplify and retransmit the signal. Each end of a segment must be terminated with a 50Ω resistor (known as a terminator).

Thick Ethernet

According to the 802.3 specification, each segment of a thick Ethernet must be no longer than 500 meters, and connections to the cable must be at least 2.5 meters apart. The cable from the Ethernet trunk to the station must be no longer than 50 meters.

Thin Ethernet

Thin Ethernet cable is equivalent to RG-58 coaxial cable. The standards specify a maximum segment length of 189 meters, a minimum distance of 0.5 meters, and no more than 30 stations. However, the 3Com Ethernet boards support a maximum segment length of 300 meters with up to 100 stations.

Fiber Optics

Ethernet can be transmitted over fiber optics. In this case the maximum segment length is 1 kilometer.

Twisted Pair

The use of twisted pair wiring with Ethernet is covered by the recently drafted 10Base-T specification.

Twisted-Pair Ethernet (10Base-T)

10Base-T is a variant of Ethernet that can run on twisted pair wiring. Since the 10Base-T standard was adopted by IEEE (the Institute of Electrical and Electronic Engineers), there has been a surge of interest and new products. As a result of the competition and the expanding market for Ethernet products, Ethernet prices in general have come down quite rapidly. 10Base-T, while a little more expensive than thin Ethernet, represents a fairly cost-effective and standardized choice.

Star Topology

10Base-T uses a star topology as shown in Figure 7-2. The network wiring terminates in a **hub** that usually has 8 to 12 connections. The network can be expanded by adding additional hubs.

Distance Limitations

10Base-T has a limit of 100 meters (328 feet) of unshielded twisted pair wire between the hub and the station.

Figure 7-2
10Base-T Design

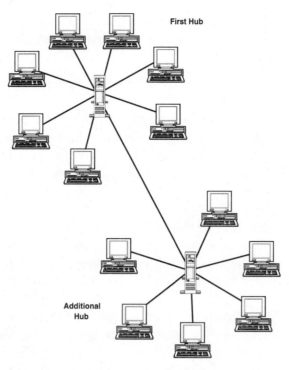

Hubs

10Base-T hubs are usually placed in a wiring center or other location that is central to the stations to be connected. Depending on the manufacturer and design, 10Base-T hubs can be interconnected using twisted pair, thin Ethernet cable, a standard coaxial Ethernet cable, or fiber optics. The hubs often provide lights or management software to indicate the status of each connection. This can be a great benefit compared to standard Ethernet.

Strengths

The use of standard twisted pair wiring is one of the major strengths of 10Base-T. This can be important when installing a network in an older building. 10Base-T uses a star topology by means of which all of the wiring comes back to a central wiring closet, making it easier to troubleshoot the network. Finally, there are options for building network management software into 10Base-T hubs. This capability provides the means to diagnose and fix network wiring and interface card problems from a central location.

Weaknesses

A disadvantage of 10Base-T is the added cost of the hardware. A network interface card may cost about $20 more than a standard (coaxial) Ethernet board, and a central hub is required. Each port on the central hub may cost about $50–$100 per connection. However, this added cost differential is decreasing because of the popularity of the new standard. The distance limitation of 100 meters between the hub and the station can also be a limiting factor. Finally, not all telephone wiring is suitable for 10Base-T.

Summary

Ethernet is a widely used standard for networking and is a safe bet for most applications. Interface cards are manufactured by scores of companies, and prices have become very competitive. Thin Ethernet uses a bus configuration that is appropriate for contiguous workgroups, but it can be difficult to troubleshoot. 10Base-T Ethernet uses a star topology with hubs that often provide network status and management information. Ethernet uses the CSMA/CD protocol, which provides an orderly way for stations to broadcast messages and handle conflicts or collisions.

Review Questions

1. How many variants of Ethernet are discussed in this unit?

* 2. Indicate at least three major differences between thin Ethernet and 10Base-T

* 3. Imagine a social gathering at which there are a number of people sitting around a table talking. What "social protocol" in this situation is analogous to the CSMA/CD protocol?

Exercises

1. If you had to link two stations that were 290 meters apart and wanted to use Ethernet, how could you connect them and what kind of components could you use?

2. Would your answer to Exercise 1 change if there were two workgroups, each with 10 people, and the workgroups were 290 meters apart?

3. Is Ethernet appropriate for your work environment or one with which you are familiar? Why?

Key Terms

Cheapernet

Collision

CSMA/CD

Ethernet

Hub

Jabber

Segment

Thin Ethernet

Unit 8 **Token Ring**

Token Ring enjoys steady popularity with more than 50 percent of all sites that have IBM or compatible mainframes using it for local area networking. Until the introduction of the 10Base-T standard for Ethernet, Token Ring was the most popular technology for new LAN installations, and it has found wide acceptance in the relatively short time that it has been available. We will indicate some of the reasons for this popularity, other than the obvious fact that it is supported by IBM.

**Learning
Objectives**

At the completion of this unit, you should be able to

1. describe the major components of a Token Ring Network,
2. list the Token Ring strengths and weaknesses,
3. appreciate how the Token Passing Protocol works,
4. understand some of the advantages of Token Ring.

Components

The hardware components of a Token Ring network include:

➡ Wiring
➡ Network Interface Card
➡ Station cable
➡ Multistation Access Unit (MAU)

These are depicted schematically in Figure 8-1 for a network with a single MAU.

**Token-Ring Wiring
Layout**

IBM includes specifications for standard Token Ring wiring as part of its **IBM Wiring Scheme**. Token Ring normally uses a high-quality shielded twisted pair wire, although it will run over unshielded twisted pair.

Figure 8-1
Token Ring Components

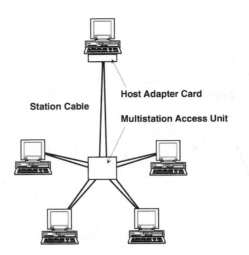

Station Cable

Host Adapter Card

Multistation Access Unit

The stations on a Token Ring network are arranged in a modified star-wired ring where each unit is connected to a Multistation Access Unit (MAU) and all of the MAUs are wired in series. This is depicted in Figure 8-2 for a single MAU.

Recommended maximum distance between the MAU and the station (or between MAUs) is 100 meters. This implies that the signal will be transmitted a maximum distance of 300 meters between one station and the next one on the ring.

Token Ring uses a "differential manchester" signal encoding scheme that is independent of polarity, hence there is no + or – lead. This eliminates the need to check polarity of wiring.

Network Interface Cards

There are two families of Token Ring network interface cards:

➡ Token Ring and Token Ring/A

➡ Token Ring 16 and Token Ring 16/A

The Token Ring and Token Ring/A cards transmit data over the network at a speed of 4Mbps. The two cards use the same protocol and speed, except that the /A model is designed for the MicroChannel bus.

Token Ring 16 NICs can operate at either 4 or 16Mbps; they employ a slightly different protocol at 16Mbps to achieve more efficient operation. The two are similar, with the Token Ring 16/A being the MicroChannel version. Either of these boards can be configured to run at a speed of 4Mbps, and operation at this speed is compatible with the earlier Token Ring adapter. However, boards operating at 16Mbps cannot be used on the same ring as boards operating at 4Mbps. Updated versions of these boards are indicated by Roman numeral II (Token Ring II).

The Token Ring MAU

The Token Ring hub or **Multistation Access Unit (MAU),** usually contains eight outlets for stations as well as ring-in and ring-out

Figure 8-2
Star-Wired Ring

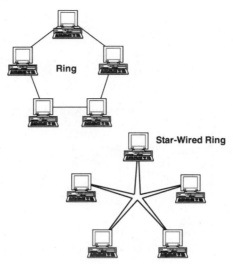

connections for wiring the hubs in series. The hub also performs a number of important functions to ensure continuous operation of a Token Ring. For example, the MAU senses when a computer is turned off and automatically bypasses the station. It also senses when a section of wire between hubs is missing and can internally reconfigure the ring-in/ring-out connections to maintain satisfactory operation.

About the Token Passing Protocol

The Token Ring Network Interface Card performs a number of sophisticated functions. In idle operation, each NIC receives information on one set of wires and transmits the same information on the other set. Since all nodes are wired in series, the information gets passed from one station to the next around the ring. When no message is being sent, stations pass a "token" to indicate that the recipient is free to convert the token to a "frame" that contains a message. This **Token Passing Protocol** supports multiple priority messages and provides a number of error detecting and reporting capabilities.

A simple analogy can help understand the operation of a Token Ring. Imagine a group of people sitting at a circular table. Each person represents a station or node on a Token Ring. Each node must remain silent until a microphone is passed to that station. That station then transmits a message of limited length and passes the microphone.

While essentially accurate, this analogy misses some of the more sophisticated features of Token Ring, such as token priority.

Strengths

Because Token Ring is an IBM product, it has become a de facto standard and is supported by a number of third-party manufacturers. In addition, the technology has some distinct advantages.

For example, Token Ring is efficient under heavy loads and allows high-priority applications to have priority. In addition, the redundant wiring scheme can correct some wiring problems, and the Token Passing Protocol has built-in measures to aid in troubleshooting.

Weaknesses

There are two primary weaknesses: cost and wiring requirements. However, there are third-party Token Ring boards that are relatively cost-effective and that can use standard unshielded twisted pair wiring.

Summary

Token Ring is quite popular in IBM circles and provides a solid, reliable networking system. Token Ring networks can handle heavy loads without bogging down and have built-in means to help correct some problems.

Review Questions

1. What is the maximum distance specified for a PC from a Token Ring hub?

* 2. Although the distance limit is quoted as between the PC and the hub, the real limiting factor is the distance between one PC and the next PC in the ring. Why is this the case?

* 3. Assuming that there is at least one PC connected to each MAU, what is the maximum distance between one PC and the next one in the ring?

* 4. With the limited information given in the discussion in this unit, can you think of anything that is inaccurate about the pass-the-microphone analogy to the Token Passing Protocol?

Exercises

1. Do a price comparison between 10Base-T and Token Ring, exclusive of wiring. Find out some typical prices for Token Ring and Ethernet NICs and typical prices for MAUs and 10Base-T hubs. Express your results in terms of both total cost for, say, 8 or 12 stations and the cost per station in each of these cases.

2. Draw a diagram with two MAUs and two computers that illustrates the answer to Review Question 3.

Key Terms

IBM Wiring Scheme

Multistation Access Unit (MAU)

Token Passing Protocol

Unit 9 **Arcnet**

The Attached Resource Computing Network, or **Arcnet**, was the first commercial product for high-speed PC networking. It was introduced in 1977 by Datapoint and gained immediate popularity. It once was the second most common networking protocol for small networks with approximately one million nodes installed. However, its popularity has been waning in recent years, especially for larger networks.

Learning Objectives

At the completion of this unit, you should be able to

1. describe the major components of Arcnet,

2. list some of the strengths and weaknesses of Arcnet,

3. appreciate the flexibility of Arcnet.

The Arcnet Token Passing Protocol

Arcnet uses a Token Passing Protocol, but unlike the way this functions in Token Ring, the stations are not wired in a ring. Instead, the signal is broadcast over the Arcnet wire, and the token is "passed" logically from one computer to the next using an algorithm to ensure that every station has a turn to transmit.

Arcnet Components

Arcnet normally uses coaxial cable and can be configured with an active hub that supports connections up to 2,000 feet from the hub. For smaller networks, a passive hub can connect up to four stations that are no more than 100 feet from the hub. In some situations it may be possible to mix active and passive hubs for added flexibility. Fiber optics can be used to interconnect stations or hubs that are up to 8,000 feet apart for a total network size of up to 20,000 feet.

Strengths

Often described as the "Volkswagen beetle" of networks, Arcnet can be a viable choice because it provides good performance and reliability at a reasonable cost. (Recent "street" prices on some Arcnet boards have dropped to well under $100.) Arcnet normally uses coaxial cable, but it can be obtained in twisted pair or fiber optics versions. The wiring topology is very flexible, permitting star and bus configurations to be mixed on the same network. It uses a reliable Token Passing Protocol and provides reasonably good performance at a speed of 2.5Mbps.

Weaknesses

One major drawback has been Arcnet's proprietary design, which, until recently, had no IEEE standard to back it up. While it uses a Token Passing Protocol, Arcnet's is not as sophisticated as the Token Ring protocol. For example, it does not allow high-priority tokens. The 2.5Mbps speed is not as robust as the 4, 10, or 16Mbps speeds available with the alternatives. Finally, Arcnet network segments are limited to 256 stations.

Summary

Arcnet provides a quite cost-effective solution for a small LAN. It is easy to set up and provides reasonable throughput under light to moderate workloads for small networks. Its growth has been hampered by the surge in popularity of Ethernet and Token Ring.

Review Questions

* 1. What type of wiring does Arcnet normally use?
* 2. What protocol does Arcnet use?
* 3. What is the largest number of stations allowed on an Arcnet segment?

Exercises

1. Price some Arcnet cards to get an indication of the market. One of the most important Arcnet vendors is Standard Micro Systems. How do its prices compare to others?

2. Do a price comparison between Arcnet and Ethernet for a network of 8 or 12 nodes. Include the cost of the NICs and the hubs, but not the wiring. Is the price of Arcnet for twisted pair significantly different from that for coaxial cable? What other factors besides price are involved in choosing between Arcnet and Ethernet?

Key Terms

Arcnet

Unit 10 **Connecting LANs to Other Computing Resources**

As networking grows within an organization, it is often necessary to interconnect two or more LANs, or to connect a departmental LAN to a central computing resource. This unit outlines some of the important options for connecting a network to other resources. As resources become interconnected, a *local* area network can become part of a larger networking scheme called a wide area network or WAN.

Learning Objectives

At the completion of this unit, you should be able to

1. understand the different types of devices that can be used to interconnect network segments,

2. appreciate the strengths and weaknesses of each interconnection option,

3. outline options for connecting to a host system,

4. appreciate the problems associated with dialing-in to a network.

Interconnecting LANs

Two separate LANs can be joined to provide a cohesive unit, or a single LAN can grow to the point where it should be organized as smaller, interconnected LANs. There are several situations in which the interconnection of LANs might be desirable. These include:

➡ Stations on the LAN are too far apart.

➡ There are too many stations.

➡ There is too much network traffic.

This section discusses some options for dealing with these potential problems.

Repeater

A **repeater** is the simplest way to interconnect LANs that use the same low-level protocol (for example, Ethernet). It is an electronic device that amplifies and conditions the signal, then retransmits it on another circuit. Repeaters can be used to extend the network beyond wiring length restrictions, to convert from one type of wiring to another, and, to a limited extent, to correct for noisy or poor wiring. Repeaters function on the physical layer of the OSI model. The advantages of repeaters include:

➡ They are relatively inexpensive and reliable since they do not perform sophisticated functions.

➡ They operate at network speeds and do not pose a bottleneck.

The disadvantages of repeaters include:

➡ They retransmit everything and, hence, do not help in heavy traffic situations.

Bridge

A **bridge** is a more sophisticated way of connecting two or more networks that use the same low-level protocol (such as Ethernet), as shown in Figure 10-1.

A bridge performs many of the same functions as a repeater, but does not retransmit every packet. It instead looks at the destination address of each packet to determine if it should be retransmitted on another segment of the network. Because of this, a bridge can be used to divide a large network into two or more subnetworks with less traffic on each part.

A bridge learns where packets must be sent by looking at the *source* address of packets that it receives. Once it receives a packet with a specific source address, then it knows where to send other packets that have the same *destination* address.

Figure 10-1
A Bridge Between Ethernet Networks

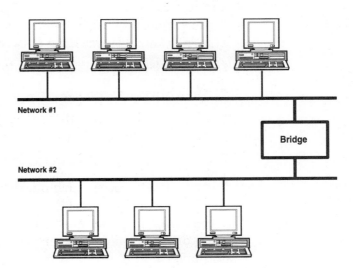

For example, if the bridge of Figure 10-1 receives a packet from address "ABC" on Network #1, it makes a note of this address as being on that network segment. Then, when it receives a packet addressed to "ABC," it knows that if the packet is on network segment #1, it need not be retransmitted onto network segment #2.

The advantages of bridges include:

➡ They can isolate traffic, and thereby can help reduce traffic on large networks.

➡ They can be programmed to exclude specific addresses and thus can provide additional network security.

➡ They can be used to connect networks that carry more than one middle layer protocol, provided that the stations at each end of a connection are using the same protocol.

The disadvantages of bridges include:

➡ They must look at addresses and process packets. This can create a bottleneck in the network.

➡ They cannot be used when there are circular or multiple paths between network segments.

A bridge operates at the data link layer of the OSI reference model.

Router

Routers provide additional capabilities on larger networks where there may be more than one path between a source and a destination. The router uses addressing information at the network layer to determine the best circuit or route by which to send each packet. This is depicted in Figure 10-2.

Because a router uses information at the network layer, it is normally used to pass packets that use a specific middle layer network protocol.

A router can connect networks that use different types of hardware. For example, a Netware server can act as an IPX router between an Ethernet and a Token Ring network.

The advantages of routers include:

➡ they can connect networks that use dissimilar low-level protocols.

➡ they can be used on large networks where there are multiple paths between points.

The disadvantages of routers include:

➡ they must process each packet and, hence, can form a bottleneck.

Gateway

A **gateway** is a complex device that is able to connect networks using different middle layer protocols. Gateways operate at the session layer and often need to function at all of the middle and lower

Figure 10-2
A Router Operates at the Network Layer

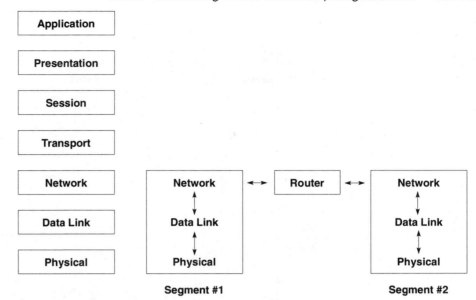

layers as well, in order to rebuild packets using a different protocol. A gateway is often used to connect a LAN to a mainframe or mini-computer host.

The advantages of gateways include:

➡ They can connect networks that use different middle-layer protocols.

The disadvantages of gateways include:

➡ They are complex and expensive and are not available for all situations.

➡ They can create a significant bottleneck.

Backbone

It is relatively common to see a situation in which a company or campus has several LANs, each of which may serve the needs of a specific lab, department, or section. In this case, it is often necessary or advantageous to connect these LANs to provide common services such as electronic mail, or to provide access to resources that are located on other LANs.

A network **backbone** is a series of wire or fiber connections that join network resources, such as departmental LANs. In most cases, users are not directly connected to a backbone, but gain indirect access to it via a bridge or a router. This indirect access helps reduce traffic on the backbone.

Figure 10-3 illustrates a backbone that connects two local Ethernets, a Token Ring, and an IBM system.

Figure 10-3
A LAN Backbone

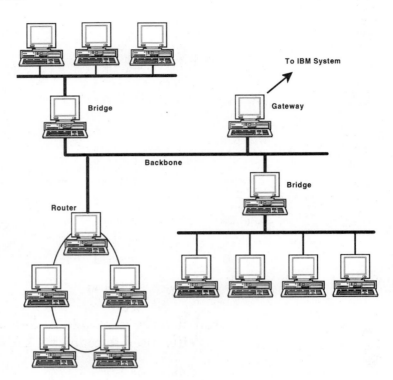

Interconnecting a LAN with a Host or a Remote User

A number of standard solutions exist for connecting a LAN to a host system (a mainframe or minicomputer) or for connecting remote personal computers to a LAN. For example, Netware SAA is a gateway product that runs on a dedicated Netware server. It provides connectivity to IBM systems along with IBM (3270) terminal emulation on a PC connected to a Netware LAN. A network can also be used to connect standard ASCII terminals to a host system.

Terminal Server

A **terminal server** is a dedicated system or a PC that acts as a link between the network and terminal ports on a central computer. The simplest type of terminal server uses standard asynchronous terminal connections on the host and can provide up to 16 connections for use by network PCs.

Any PC on the network can use the terminal server to connect to a terminal port on the host system and can employ a terminal emulation program to communicate with the host. This is a flexible way to provide occasional users with access to computing resources and does not require a one-to-one relationship between users and ports on the central system.

A typical terminal server arrangement is illustrated in Figure 10-4. In this case, any four of the eight PCs can use one of the ports to the mainframe.

Figure 10-4
Terminal Server

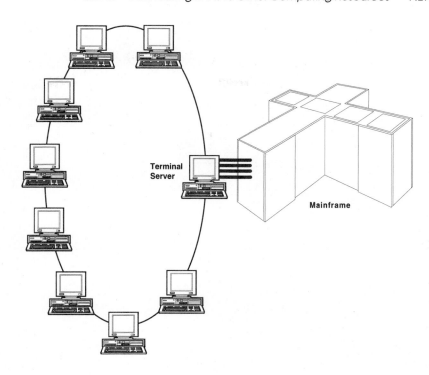

Another type of terminal server is used in a TCP/IP environment to allow workstations to connect to a host via an Ethernet connection. In this case, the workstation uses the TELNET program (usually included with TCP/IP) to emulate a standard terminal.

Remote Access

It is often the case that users want **remote access** to a LAN from home or other sites. Dialing in over a phone line to use a LAN can present a special kind of problem associated with the different speeds of communication. In particular, a phone line is about a thousand times slower than a LAN.

To avoid this dial-in bottleneck, a special **access server** can be set up on the LAN to provide dial-up access, as shown in Figure 10-5. The user dials into the access server and takes control of it, using a remote control program. The access server is a computer that is physically connected to the network and carries out most of the processing. Only the keyboard input and screen images are sent over the phone line to the remote user.

The Novell Netware Access Server is both software and hardware that can be installed on a standard PC to provide up to eight or so dial-up connections. (The theoretical limit is 15, but performance is sluggish with more than 8.)

Figure 10-5
Access Server

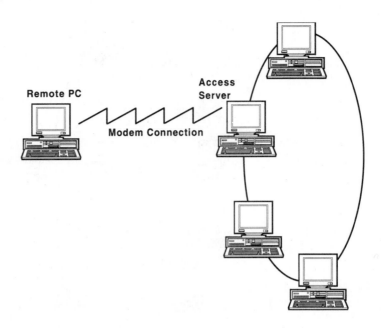

TCP/IP Interconnect

The Transmission Control Protocol (TCP) and the Internet Protocol (IP), together with FTP (File Transfer Protocol), SMTP (Simple Mail Transfer Protocol), and TELNET (Terminal Emulation), constitute a standard originally promoted by the Department of Defense for use on the experimental packet-switching network ARPANET. TCP/IP now enjoys wide acceptance and use, especially in academic environments. Because of the certification required by the government and almost universal support by vendors, TCP/IP provides an effective method of interconnecting a diverse variety of PCs and minicomputers or mainframes running different operating systems.

In addition, the TCP/IP suite of applications often includes network management using a scheme called **SNMP** (Simple Network Management Protocol).

Summary

Networks can be interconnected in a number of ways. At the lowest level, two or more networks can be connected via a repeater. This makes them behave as one larger network. A bridge can also link two or more networks and in so doing help reduce network traffic on each segment by filtering packets that are "local." In the Novell environment, a Netware server can act as a router to connect segments that use different lower-level protocols such as Ethernet or Token Ring. A server running Netware 3.11 or later can act as a gateway to connect users to IBM resources, while a terminal server can provide access to terminal ports on a central system. Finally, an access server can provide dial-in access to a LAN.

Review Questions

* **1.** List some of the differences between a repeater and a bridge.

2. Name some differences between a bridge and a router.

* **3.** Arrange the following in order of increasing functionality and complexity: bridge, gateway, repeater, router.

4. What are the two types of terminal server that are mentioned in the text?

* **5.** Why are there special problems when a user wishes to connect to a network via a phone line?

Exercises

1. The text indicates that a bridge can help reduce network traffic on each segment. Represent this by drawing a diagram of a network with a bridge that joins two busy LANs where the user situation is such that there is little or *no* traffic across the bridge.

2. At the other extreme, a bridge can be of little or no help in a situation where it is not properly positioned on the network and all or most packets need to be forwarded across the bridge. Draw a diagram of a network and a user situation where virtually *all* network traffic is passed across a bridge.

3. A number of remote control programs allow you to use a phone line and modems to connect two computers so that one is controlling the other. (These include NetRemote, Carbon Copy, PC Anywhere, and CO/Session.) Use of a remote control program represents the simplest way to provide remote access to a LAN. Draw a diagram to illustrate this.

4. If you were setting up a terminal server to provide Netware users with access to a central host, where would you be most likely to place the terminal server hardware?

Key Terms

Access server

Backbone

Bridge

FTP

Gateway

Remote access

Repeater

Router

SNMP

Terminal server

Unit 11 **Introduction to Novell Netware**

The local area network market has been growing rapidly for the last five years, with a growth rate of more than 30 percent per year. Novell Netware is an important component of this growth. Netware accounts for well over 50 percent of the market, and its growth has outpaced the industry. This unit is an introduction to this important network operating system.

Learning Objectives

At the completion of this unit, you should be able to

1. identify the major features of Netware,
2. understand the DOS-like services provided by a network,
3. login to a Novell server and connect to a network printer,
4. set up logical drives.

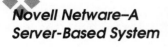

Network Operating System

A network operating system provides the resources that makes a network function properly. Through the network operating system, multiple users are given access to shared printers, resources, and data stored on the network. The network operating system also provides security against unauthorized use of resources.

Novell Netware–A Server-Based System

With the exception of Personal Netware, which is a peer-to-peer system, Novell Netware is a server-based network operating system that utilizes a file server to provide resources to users on the network. In contrast, a peer-to-peer operating system such as Personal Netware or Windows for Workgroups allows any station on the network to provide services.

Netware 2

Netware 2 is the "classic" version of Netware. The latest releases (2.2 and later) consolidate the previous versions into one family of software, the only difference being the number of users supported (5,

10, 50, or 100). The earlier versions included Entry Level System (ELS), Advanced, and System Fault Tolerant (SFT). Netware 2.2 and later versions incorporate the features previously found in the former SFT Netware, including the capability to duplex hard disks and controllers for improved **fault tolerance**. In addition, these versions have been modified to be more consistent with many of the new features of Netware 3. Netware 2 is appropriate when you wish to get the most of limited server resources. It is proven technology that can run on a 286 or a 386 system with as little as 2.5MB of memory. It can be set up in a nondedicated configuration where the server can also be used as a workstation.

Netware 3

Netware 3 is the first of a new family of Netware that is optimized to take advantage of the capabilities of 386 and 486 processors. It can integrate all of the most important desktop operating systems, including DOS, OS/2, UNIX, and Macintosh, and in addition it supports protocols such as AppleTalk and TCP/IP. Netware 3 requires a minimum of a 386 system with 4MB of memory. It is available in versions for 5, 10, 20, 50, 100, or 250 users.

Netware 4

The newest version of Netware represents a major shift in emphasis away from a *server-based* system to a *service-based* system. It includes advanced capabilities for multiple-server environments such as global directories of names and resources and network auditing services.

Netware Directory Services

Netware Directory Services (**NDS**) is a global directory of names and services in the Netware 4 environment. NDS includes all network names and resources organized into a hierarchical database that usually includes an **organization** (O) such as a company or school, an **organizational unit** (OU) such as a department or location and **common names** (CN) for users and resources within the organizational unit. The network administrator creates the NDS to reflect the network and organizational structure. Once set up, all users and resources refer to the same NDS structure everywhere on the network. For example, if the organization is STATEU, the organizational unit is SCIENCE, and the common name (user name) is JSMITH, then JSMITH is known as .JSMITH.SCIENCE.STATEU throughout the network. The explicit representation is:

```
.CN=JSMITH.OU=SCIENCE.O=STATEU
```

Netware, a Specialized Operating System

Netware is a single-purpose operating system that provides a lean, efficient way to provide file sharing, print sharing, and other network functions. With it, a single PC can handle the needs of 20, 50, 100, or even 250 or more users. Netware runs on a variety of PC platforms and supports a wide range of hardware boards and protocols.

The Novell strategy is to use a proprietary, specialized operating system that can be optimized to provide network services. In contrast, most of the other networking solutions use a standard operating system such as UNIX or OS/2. These operating systems sometimes require a greater memory and processor "overhead" in order to run, and, hence, may require a more powerful system to serve a given-sized network.

Other Capabilities of Netware

Netware, like all of the major network operating systems, provides basic print and file sharing capabilities as outlined above. In addition, a network server might provide some of the following capabilities.

Electronic Mail

Electronic mail, or E-mail, is a popular network application that can enhance communication between network users. Versions of Netware before Netware 4 provide only the most rudimentary mail capabilities. Netware 4 provides some additional support for the Simple Mail Transport Protocol (SMTP). Nevertheless, most Novell network managers provide a third-party electronic mail system.

Remote Access

As indicated earlier, some special problems are associated with dialing in to a LAN. Novell and other vendors provide remote access options for dealing with these problems.

Internal Routing

A Netware server can act as a router between two or more networks. This capability is built into Netware and can also be set up in a dedicated PC.

Fault Tolerance

The Novell operating systems can be set up to survive a disk or controller malfunction without loss of data. This is done through the use of disk duplexing or through a third-party RAID system. Novell Netware also supports full server duplexing where two servers are in parallel operation and the network can continue to function after the loss of any component in either system. This capability is referred to as System Fault Tolerance level 3 (or SFT III).

Network Administration Tools

Every network operating system should provide tools for administering the network. Most operating systems provide these as menu-driven utilities. Netware 4 also provides Windows-based graphical administration tools called NEUSER and NWADMIN. These tools are important factors in ensuring the continued success of the network.

Diagnostic Utilities

Analyzing network problems can be very difficult. Unfortunately, Novell and other systems do not include particularly good diagnostic utilities. However, they can be purchased as an option (LANalyzer) or from third parties.

Security

Security is one of the most important aspects of managing a network, especially with applications that use sensitive personnel or financial data. Netware offers good system security, as we will see in Units 14 and 18.

Network Management Systems

Network management systems often include the capability to obtain accurate information about the status of servers, adapter cards, wiring centers, and other components of the network. (Network management used in this context should not be confused with the process of managing a LAN.) This type of network management capability is invaluable in troubleshooting a large network that may span several buildings. Both Netware 3 and Netware 4 have the "hooks" to allow inclusion of network management. In addition, Netware 4 includes the Netware Services Manager and Network Management Agents to monitor the network and provide a Netware Management Map. Netware 4 also provides support for the industry-standard Simple Network Management Protocol (SNMP).

The Novell File Server

Novell's file server provides resources such as mass storage and shared printers. These are made available to individual users by making the server resources look like resources attached to your local system. For example, a network printer is made to look as if it were attached to a local printer port on the PC, or a drive is made to look as if it were a local hard disk. Remember that because Netware is a specialized operating system, it must act like a DOS system to make its resources look familiar to a DOS user. Similarly, if you are using a Macintosh computer, the Netware server must act like an Apple system to make *its* resources look familiar.

Starting Up and Shutting Down the File Server

Once a server is properly configured, starting it up is usually a matter of turning it on. When the server is running, it will normally display a colon (:) as a console prompt, indicating that it is ready to receive a console command. However, there are some differences in starting and stopping a server and in using the server console, depending on the version of Netware and the options used to install it.

Starting a 3.x or 4.x Server

All 3.x and 4.x servers are set up to boot in two stages. First, DOS is loaded from the hard drive or from a floppy disk, and then the server program is loaded. The server program switches the processor to protected mode and loads additional Netware drivers or Netware

Loadable Modules (NLMs) to add system features. All of these features can be added or removed as the server is running, but it is normal to set up the server with an AUTOEXEC.NCF file that loads all resources automatically. (The AUTOEXEC.NCF file is discussed in the next unit.)

Starting a 2.x Server

A dedicated Netware 2 server will automatically boot from the hard disk and load the operating system when you turn the server on. As the system loads, you will see status messages on the monitor. If Value Added Processes (VAPs) have been added to a Netware 2.x server, you will be given the option to load them.

Starting a Nondedicated Server

In some cases, a Netware 2.x server will be set up as a nondedicated server so that it can also be used as a workstation. In this case, the server is set up so that it boots automatically from a floppy or a hard disk. The >**CONSOLE** and the :**DOS** commands can be used at the server console to switch between the DOS workstation mode and the Novell server mode.

Note *The > and : are not part of the command, but are used to indicate that the DOS prompt should be present when you enter the CONSOLE command and that the console prompt should be present when you enter the DOS command.*

Startup Messages

As a Netware server starts up, various messages will be displayed on the console. Occasionally, you may notice an error message. If this happens, make a note of it and inform your network administrator. In most cases, the server will continue on past the error. The network administrator can review the error log later.

Shutting Down a Server

If you know that all users have logged out, simply enter the :**DOWN** command (type **DOWN** at the file server console). The system will be shut down and you can turn the power off. You may need to use the >**USERLIST** command to see a list of all users currently logged into the network. Warn them and ask them to "logout" using the :**BROAD-CAST <message>** command, where the message might be something like "Server will be shut down in 10 minutes, please logout." In the meantime, you can prevent new users from logging in, by using the :**DISABLE LOGINS** command. When you enter the DOWN command Netware will warn you in the event that server files are in use and will give you a second chance not to bring the server down. However, do not rely on this. You can shut a server down without getting this warning message, but still leave users "hanging" in the middle of an application, and unable to save their current work.

Login

Before you can use the resources on a network, you must "login" or connect to the file server as a specific user. Once you have done this, you have rights to use designated resources. Logging into a file server presupposes that several things have taken place:

➡ The server has been started, as outlined in the previous paragraphs.

➡ You are using a PC with a properly configured network card that has been physically connected to the network, as outlined in Unit 4.

➡ The network shell programs have been loaded to establish a connection to the server (also outlined in Unit 4).

Login Process

Once you have booted the system and loaded the network shell files, begin the login process by changing to the network login directory, usually represented as drive F:. Do this, as usual, by typing **F:** at the DOS prompt. Next, issue the **>LOGIN** command by typing **LOGIN** or **LOGIN <username>**.

Once again, these steps may have been incorporated into your AUTO-EXEC.BAT file, the STARTNET.BAT file, or a custom network interface program.

When the login process has started, the server will prompt you for a **username** if you have not already provided it with one, and will ask you for a **password**. You cannot login unless both the username and the password are correct.

Login Process with Two or More Servers

The process is the same as above, except that you may need to specify the server you wish to login to. You can do this by specifying the server name as well as the username in the form **<server>/ <username>**. For example, to log onto server NET as user JSMITH, you can type the command

>**LOGIN NET/JSMITH**

Alternatively, you can type **LOGIN** and then type **NET/JSMITH** in response to the "Enter your login name" prompt.

Logging In to Two or More Servers

Once you have logged onto a server, you can log onto a Netware 2.x or 3.x server at the same time using the **>ATTACH <server>** command. In most cases, you will be asked to type a username and password. If you are in a Netware 4 environment, the Netware Directory Services makes resources on all Netware 4 servers available through a single login.

In this case, you may need to type your full network user name (depending on where you login). For example, for the same NDS structure indicated above, you would login, using

```
LOGIN .JSMITH.SCIENCE.STATEU
```

Setting or Changing Your Password

One of the first things you might want to do after logging in for the first time is to change your password using the **SETPASS** command. An easy way to do this is to type **SETPASS** at the DOS prompt. You will be prompted to type first your current password, and then the new password. The new password must be typed correctly twice in a row before it takes effect.

Using Network Mass Storage

A network server can provide an enormous amount of storage space that can be accessed and shared by network users. Novell Netware provides its own way of organizing this storage space.

Netware Volumes

The term **volume** usually refers to all or part of a server hard disk that is available for use over the network. The volume is a logical unit that can be one or more hard disks or a part of a hard disk. The primary volume is always given the name SYS. Other volumes can be given any name like VOL1 or APPS. The volume on a netware server is analogous to a hard disk in DOS and can be organized into directories and subdirectories, just like a local drive. Because volumes are visible everywhere on a Netware 4 network, the server name is pre-pended to the volume name with the underscore character. Thus, volumes SYS, VOL1, and APPS on the NET server are called NET_SYS, NET_VOL1, and NET_APPS respectively.

Network Drive Designations

Normally, DOS reserves drive letters A: through E: for local floppy disks and hard disks, while the storage on a Netware server normally appears as drive F: or above. As a result, the Netware volume can be made to appear as if it were drive F: on your PC. The association between a Netware volume and a drive letter is made using the Netware >**MAP** command. Because the association is done by the network software, it can be changed. That is, at one time drive F: could be associated with a specific network volume, and at another time it could be associated with a different network volume.

The MAP Command

The Netware >MAP command allows a specific directory or subdirectory within a volume on the server's hard disk to be associated with a drive letter. For example, drive G: could be associated with the subdirectory WPERF of the APPS directory on the disk volume SYS on the file server NET, using the following MAP command:

```
MAP G:=NET/SYS:APPS\WPERF
```

Once this is done, drive G: "points to" the directory \APPS\WPERF of the SYS volume on the file server NET. With Netware 4, the same syntax or the following format will often work (depending on where you are attached to the network):

```
MAP G:=NET_SYS:APPS\WPERF
```

However, the explicit format includes the organizational unit and organization to which the server volume belongs. For example, if server NET is assigned to the ENGLISH department at STATEU, the format is:

```
MAP G:=.NET_SYS.ENGLISH.STATEU:APPS\WPERF
```

Similarities to a Local Drive

Once a portion of the network hard disk is represented as a drive letter such as F:, it can be used almost as if you had a hard disk in your PC. Nearly all of the DOS commands such as DIR, COPY, and the like can be applied to the network drive and will produce the expected outcome. Understandably, there are some DOS commands such as CHKDSK and FORMAT that will not work on a network drive.

Accessing a Drive

An important difference between a local drive and a network drive is that *you must have been given access to a network drive before you can use it*. This is discussed in more detail in the next unit.

Changing the Mapping

Once a network drive letter has been established using the MAP command, the drive mapping can be changed to a different directory using the DOS CD (or CHDIR) command. For example:

```
G:
CD \APPS
```

will associate drive G: with the SYS:APPS directory, in the same way that CD will change the directory path for a local disk drive.

Fake Roots

A special form of the MAP command can be used to make a directory or subdirectory act as if it were the root directory of a drive letter. To use this capability, add the word ROOT after the MAP command. For example:

```
MAP ROOT I:=NET/SYS:USERS\JANE
```

Now, the user will not be able to use CD to change to a higher level directory on drive I: (such as USERS) because USERS\JANE acts as if it were the root directory of the volume. This capability is useful when running Windows in the network environment.

Figure 11-1
CAPTURE Redirects Printer Output

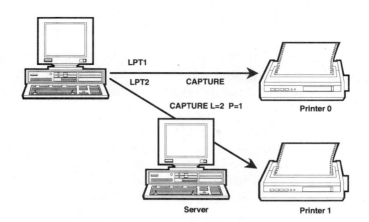

Using Network Print Queues

A network **print queue** acts as a print buffer between your computer and a network printer. It collects output from your system and stores it until it is ready to be printed. For example, if you are using a word processing program and send a document to be printed on a network printer, the output from your system is redirected to a print queue for temporary storage. When the document is completely sent to the queue, it will then be given a place in line to be printed on the network printer. Usually, the document begins to print at that time.

Similarities to a Local Printer

Using the Netware **CAPTURE** command, your local PC can be connected to a network printer via a print queue. Once this has been done, the network printer will appear to be connected to your PC as far as most PC software is concerned.

As shown in Figure 11-1, a printer attached to a server can be logically associated with, say, the first printer port (LPT1:) on your computer. Once this has been done, the software that you run on your computer will think that you have a printer attached to LPT1:. Netware takes care of redirecting the output from your computer to the network printer. Alternatively, a network printer can be associated with the second printer port (LPT2:) on your computer. In this case, your software would see a printer attached to LPT2: and Netware would take care of sending the output to the appropriate network printer.

Differences Between Using a Local and a Network Printer

There are some differences between using a locally attached printer and a network printer. First, the printed output from a network printer may take longer to appear than the printed output from a local one. This is primarily because a document will not start printing until all of it has been sent to the print queue. On the other hand, you can quickly send a document to the network print queue and continue working on something else. Although the total time to print a document is longer, it usually takes less time to send the document to the queue than it would to print it locally.

A network printer can also be more complicated to use, since there is at least one additional step. However, the network administrator can ordinarily create menus or automate this process.

Connecting to a Network Printer Using CAPTURE

As indicated above, you can use the Netware CAPTURE command to assign a network printer to a local printer port. The most direct method is to simply type the word **CAPTURE**. This uses the current printer defaults and will normally redirect printer output from LPT1: to network printer 0. You can also use the CAPTURE command with the parameters L=# and Q=<name> to specify the local printer port (L) and the network queue name (Q). For example:

```
CAPTURE L=2 Q=Laser
```

redirects print output from the second local printer port (LPT2:) to the network queue called LASER. Once output has been redirected in this way, all normal printer output that would have gone to the captured printer port (LPT1: or LPT2:) is instead sent to the network queue.

There are many variations to the CAPTURE command. For example, you can specify that a job is printed after 30 seconds of inactivity (`ti=30`) or that no banner page is printed (`nb`). However, the PRINTCON utility provides an easier way to accomplish the same thing.

Using PRINTCON

PRINTCON is a Novell utility that can be used to customize your CAPTURE command. Briefly, you can use the PRINTCON utility to set up defaults for the CAPTURE command and can also set up custom options. For example, you can create a configuration called COLOR to print to a color printer. Once this has been done, you can redirect printer output using CAPTURE (for default settings) and CAPTURE J=COLOR for custom options (in this case, sending output to the color printer). The use of the PRINTCON utility is discussed in the next unit.

Printing to a Local Printer

If you do not use the CAPTURE command, you can print to a local printer by simply printing as usual. If you are attached to a network printer using the same port as the local printer, use the **ENDCAP** command to return to using the local printer. Use the form **ENDCAP L=#** to deactivate capturing from a specific local printer port number.

CAPTURE SH

When in doubt, use the form **CAPTURE SH** to "show" or display the current status of the print ports. This will display a list of print ports and detail the queues to which they are currently being redirected.

Netware Commands

There are several classes of Netware commands. These include: DOS-like Netware commands that are entered from the DOS prompt (>) and carry out an action; Netware menu utility commands that are also entered at the DOS prompt but bring up a specialized menu system; and console commands that are entered at the server console. Netware 4 also features GUI utilities that are invoked from within Windows. Netware menu utility commands are discussed in the next unit.

Network Versions of DOS Commands

There are a few special commands that provide alternatives and/or network extensions to some of the DOS commands. These include **NCOPY**, **NDIR**, and **NPRINT**.

NCOPY is very similar to the DOS XCOPY command but is more "aware" of special network characteristics of files stored on the server. NDIR can be used much like the DOS DIR command, but also has features to show network attributes of files or directories. NPRINT is similar to the DOS PRINT command but sends output to a network printer.

Other Netware Commands

Other netware commands include >**WHOAMI** to provide information about whom you are logged in as, >**USERLIST** to display a list of users logged onto the network, and >**SLIST** (NDIR in Netware 4) to see a list of servers attached to the network.

Using the Console

You can carry out a number of network management and monitoring tasks at the network console. However, the use of the 2.x console is basically different from the use of the 3.x and 4.x console.

The 2.x Server Console

A 2.x dedicated server always shows the console prompt, while a nondedicated server may need to be switched to console mode using the >CONSOLE command from the DOS prompt. Type **:MONITOR** to see the activity at six stations, along with server load and information about the version of Netware. Issue the **CONFIG** command by typing **:CONFIG** to display a summary of the way that the network is set up (NIC configurations and drive setups). If core printing services are used, the **:PRINTER** and **:QUEUE** commands are used to set up and configure printers and queues. This is discussed in more detail in the next unit.

The 3.x and 4.x Server Console

In contrast to Netware 2, virtually all features of Netware 3 and 4 can be added, removed, and reconfigured at the console while the server is in operation. Many features are added or removed using the **:LOAD** or **:UNLOAD** command. For example, **:LOAD MONITOR** will bring up a menu that allows you to view network activity and perform a number of management functions. Similarly, `:LOAD PSERVER <name>` will start a print server process. Other console features of Netware 3 and 4 are discussed in the coming sections.

Netware 3 and 4 are multitasking operating systems. Therefore, there can be many processes running, only one of which can be viewed at any one time. Use the [Alt]-[Esc] key combination to cycle from one process to the next, or use [Ctrl]-[Alt]-[Esc] to select from a list of server processes.

Summary

With the exception of Personal Netware, Netware is a server-based operating system that provides access to shared resources such as printers, hard disks, data, and software applications. Netware 2 is a "lean and mean" system, while Netware 3 provides additional capabilities and functions for larger networks. Netware 4 contains all of the features of Netware 3 and also has data management and the global Netware Directory Services aimed at the large enterprise that may have multiple servers.

Each user must login to the network using a username and a password. The network supervisor must give specific access to server resources before they can be used. Once authorized, a user can access specific portions of the network drive just like a DOS drive. Similarly, Netware users can easily connect to network printers using the CAPTURE command.

Netware is designed to operate much like DOS and recognizes most of the appropriate DOS commands. In addition, it has some Netware-specific commands that extend the DOS capabilities.

Review Questions

1. List some of the functions and capabilities of a network operating system. Which do you think are most important?

* 2. Describe the login process. What would you check if you typed `LOGIN` and got a response "Bad Command or Filename"?

* 3. Briefly list some of the similarities and differences between a local hard disk (drive C:) and a network drive (drive G:).

* 4. Describe the effect of the CAPTURE command. What role does the PRINTCON utility play here?

Exercises

1. Obtain a username and password from your instructor and LOGIN to a network. Once logged in:

   a. Use the >SETPASS command to change your password.

  b. Use >CAPTURE and >CAPTURE SH to redirect output to a network printer and view the configuration.

2. Use the commands: >IPX I, >WHOAMI, >USERLIST /A, NDIR, and >SLIST to determine as much as you can about the configuration of your network. (Use the format **NDIR /?** for help.)

3. With appropriate authorization, shut down and restart a Netware server.

Key Terms

ATTACH <server>

BROADCAST <message>

CAPTURE

Common name

CONFIG

CONSOLE

DISABLE LOGINS

DOS command

DOWN

ENDCAP

Fault tolerance

LOAD

LOGIN

MAP

NCOPY

NDIR

NDS

NPRINT

Organization

Organizational unit

Password

Print queue

PRINTCON

PRINTER

QUEUE

SETPASS

SLIST

UNLOAD

USERLIST

Username

Volume

WHOAMI

Unit 12 The Novell Menu Utilities

The Novell menu system provides a variety of network management capabilities. With Netware 4, the menu utilities have been reorganized and expanded to reflect the new capabilities of this environment. The following discussion focuses on the versions available with Netware 2 and 3. Later, we will indicate the new features of the Netware 4 menu system.

A specific menu can be accessed by typing the appropriate command (**FILER**, **VOLINFO**, and so on) or can be selected from a master menu.

Learning Objectives

At the completion of this unit, you should be able to

1. use the Novell menu system,
2. add a user (with appropriate authorization),
3. change your password using SYSCON.

The Novell Master Menu

The Novell Master Menu provides access to all of the Novell menu utilities. To start the master menu, login to the server and type **MENU MAIN** at the DOS prompt. It provides access to the eight Novell menu utilities, as shown in Figure 12-1.

Using the Novell Menus

All of the Novell menus operate in much the same way: highlight a selection, press Enter to activate the selection, or press Esc to "back out" or to leave a menu.

There are two ways to highlight a selection: use the ↑ or ↓ keys, or press the key corresponding to the first character of the selection—in this case, one of the number keys.

Figure 12-1
The Main Menu

```
┌──────────────────────────────────┐
│             Main Menu            │
├──────────────────────────────────┤
│                                  │
│   1.  Session Management         │
│   2.  File Management            │
│   3.  Volume Information         │
│   4.  System Configuration       │
│   5.  File Server Monitoring     │
│   6.  Print Queue Management      │
│   7.  Print Job Configurations   │
│   8.  Printer Definitions        │
│   9.  Logout                     │
│                                  │
└──────────────────────────────────┘
```

SESSION

The Session Management menu, or **SESSION**, shown in Figure 12-2, provides information about what is currently happening on the server. This includes which drive letters are assigned to specific directories, which directories will be searched when a command file must be located, which user groups are defined, and which users are currently on the network.

Figure 12-2
The Session Management Menu

```
┌──────────────────────────────────┐
│         Available Topics         │
├──────────────────────────────────┤
│                                  │
│   Change Current Server          │
│   Drive Mappings                 │
│   Group List                     │
│   Search Mappings                │
│   Select Default Drive           │
│   User List                      │
│                                  │
└──────────────────────────────────┘
```

FILER

The File Management menu, illustrated in Figure 12-3, provides information about the directories and files on the system. **FILER** can also be used to copy files or to set restrictions on use of files.

Figure 12-3
The File Management Menu

```
┌──────────────────────────────────┐
│         Available Topics         │
├──────────────────────────────────┤
│                                  │
│   Current Directory Information  │
│   Directory Contents             │
│   Select Current Directory       │
│   Set Filer Options              │
│   Volume Information             │
│                                  │
└──────────────────────────────────┘
```

Figure 12-4
The VOLINFO Screen

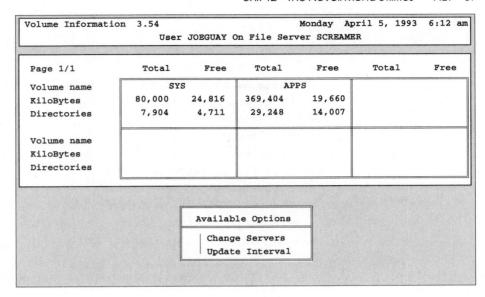

```
Volume Information  3.54                    Monday  April 5, 1993   6:12 am
                        User JOEGUAY On File Server SCREAMER


Page 1/1              Total      Free     Total      Free     Total      Free

Volume name              SYS                  APPS
KiloBytes           80,000    24,816    369,404    19,660
Directories          7,904     4,711     29,248    14,007


Volume name
KiloBytes
Directories




                            Available Options

                            Change Servers
                            Update Interval
```

VOLINFO

The Volume Information menu, shown in Figure 12-4, provides exact details on the amount of disk storage available. **VOLINFO** displays disk space used and available for each disk volume.

SYSCON

The System Configuration menu shown in Figure 12-5 is the most useful for managing the network. **SYSCON** can be used to create users and manage user rights. It can also be used to create user login scripts and to set restrictions on use.

Figure 12-5
The System Configuration Menu

```
          Available Topics

Accounting
Change Current Server
File Server Information
Group Information
Supervisor Options
User Information
```

FCONSOLE

The File Server Monitoring menu shown in Figure 12-6 provides tools for managing the server and displays statistics on its use. It can also be used to shut the server down or set the server date and time (under the Status option). The following diagram shows the Netware 2 **FCONSOLE** screen with asterisks after the menu choices that are not present in the Netware 3 version of FCONSOLE. Most of these missing functions are available in the

Figure 12-6
*The File Server Monitoring
Menu*

```
┌─────────────────────────────────────┐
│          Available Options           │
│                                      │
├─────────────────────────────────────┤
│  Broadcast Console Message           │
│  Change Current File Server          │
│  Connection Information              │
│  Down File Server                    │
│  File/Lock Activity*                 │
│  LAN Driver Information*             │
│  Purge All Salvageable Files*        │
│  Statistics*                         │
│  Status                              │
│  Version Information                 │
└─────────────────────────────────────┘
```

MONITOR NLM and through the remote console feature of Netware 3 and 4.

PCONSOLE

The Print Console menu illustrated in Figure 12-7, or **PCONSOLE**, can be used to manage print queues and print servers. This includes creating, deleting, or renaming print queues; controlling print jobs; creating, deleting or renaming print servers; configuring printers and print servers; and assigning print queue operators and users.

Figure 12-7
The Print Console Menu

```
┌─────────────────────────────────────┐
│          Available Options           │
│                                      │
├─────────────────────────────────────┤
│  Change Current File Server          │
│  Print Queue Information             │
│  Print Server Information            │
└─────────────────────────────────────┘
```

PRINTCON

The Print Job Configurations menu shown in Figure 12-8 allows users to customize how printing jobs are sent to a print queue. **PRINTCON** enables each user to create and name one or more print configurations that specify parameters such as the local printer port, the network printer, and setup strings that are sent to the printer.

Figure 12-8
*The Print Job
Configurations Menu*

```
┌─────────────────────────────────────┐
│           Available Topics           │
│                                      │
├─────────────────────────────────────┤
│  Edit Print Job Configurations       │
│  Select Default Print Job Configuration │
│  Supervisor-Copy Print Job Configurations │
└─────────────────────────────────────┘
```

PRINTDEF

The Printer Definitions utility shown in Figure 12-9 allows the creation of a print device (such as an Epson FX80 printer) and standard modes (for example, condensed) and forms. The **PRINTDEF** option chosen can then be used in conjunction with PRINTCON to customize the way in which each user sends files to a printer.

Figure 12-9
*The Printer Definition
Utility*

```
┌─────────────────────────────┐
│  PrintDef Options           │
├─────────────────────────────┤
│  Print Devices              │
│  Forms                      │
└─────────────────────────────┘
```

SYSCON Example

The following System Configuration examples illustrate the User Information submenu of the SYSCON menu.

Figure 12-10
*The System Configurations
Menu*

```
┌─────────────────────────────┐
│     Available Topics        │
├─────────────────────────────┤
│  Accounting                 │
│  Change Current Server      │
│  File Server Information     │
│  Group Information           │
│  Supervisor Options          │
│  User Information            │
└─────────────────────────────┘
```

For the first example, shown in Figure 12-10, bring up the SYSCON menu by typing **SYSCON** at the DOS prompt. Select the User Information option to bring up a list of USERS defined on the network. Select your user name and press ⏎Enter to summon the menu shown in Figure 12-11.

Figure 12-11
*The User Information
Submenu*

```
┌─────────────────────────────┐
│     User Information        │
├─────────────────────────────┤
│  Account Restrictions       │
│  Change Password            │
│  Full Name                  │
│  Groups Belonged To         │
│  Login Script               │
│  Other Information          │
│  Security Equivalences      │
│  Station Restrictions       │
│  Time Restrictions          │
│  Trustee Assignments        │
└─────────────────────────────┘
```

Now select Change Password to change your password, using the menu system instead of the SETPASS command. As with SETPASS, you will be prompted to type in your new password (twice, to verify that you have made no typing mistakes).

Select Login Script to bring up an edit window where you can create or edit your own custom login script to automate tasks, much like an AUTOEXEC.BAT file does when you start DOS.

Automating Tasks Using a Login Script

Netware provides two levels of custom login scripts. The first, a system login script, is much like an AUTOEXEC.BAT file for everyone logging into the network. The second level of login script, user, is accessed as shown above using the User Information option on the SYSCON menu. The user login script, once defined, is executed after the system login script. You can create or edit your personal user login script using an editor screen that comes up when you select the Login Script option. Some commonly used login script commands are given in Appendix A.

For example, network user JOE can issue the following commands in the login script to associate drive I: with his personal directory HOME\JOE and to make it the current one:

```
MAP I:=SYS:\HOME\JOE
DRIVE I:
```

Setting Up a Print Job Configuration

A print job configuration establishes a number of parameters associated with printing. These include the local print port, the network print queue, and the type of banner sheet that will be printed. You can use the PRINTCON menu utility to create or edit one or more print job configurations and to establish a default configuration.

PRINTCON Example

Type PRINTCON at the DOS prompt or type MENU MAIN to bring up the main Novell menu and select the Print Job Configuration option. This brings up the main PRINTCON menu shown in Figure 12-8.

Normally, you would select Edit Print Job Configurations to create or change a configuration.

You should see a list of the current print job configurations. Press [Ins] to create a new configuration file and type the configuration name—say, HOLD. The Edit Print Job Configuration "HOLD" screen shown in Figure 12-12 should appear. Go through this screen and select options that are appropriate for your needs. At each option, you can press [Enter] and, if appropriate, you will see a list of possibilities.

Figure 12-12
The Print Job Configuration Screen

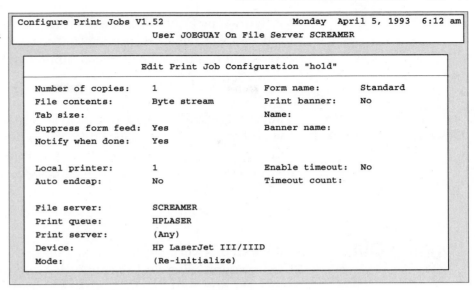

```
Configure Print Jobs V1.52                Monday  April 5, 1993  6:12 am
                    User JOEGUAY On File Server SCREAMER

        ┌──────────────────────────────────────────────────────────┐
        │               Edit Print Job Configuration "hold"         │
        │                                                            │
        │  Number of copies:    1              Form name:    Standard│
        │  File contents:       Byte stream    Print banner: No      │
        │  Tab size:                           Name:                 │
        │  Suppress form feed:  Yes            Banner name:          │
        │  Notify when done:    Yes                                  │
        │                                                            │
        │                                                            │
        │  Local printer:       1              Enable timeout: No     │
        │  Auto endcap:         No             Timeout count:        │
        │                                                            │
        │  File server:         SCREAMER                             │
        │  Print queue:         HPLASER                              │
        │  Print server:        (Any)                                │
        │  Device:              HP LaserJet III/IIID                 │
        │  Mode:                (Re-initialize)                      │
        └──────────────────────────────────────────────────────────┘
```

Here are some of the options available for setting up your print job configuration and how they are best used:

Suppress Form Feed

Select Yes if your application always sends a form feed at the end of a print job. Otherwise, the printer will always output a blank page at the end of the job. Select No if you are using an application like dBASE that does not send a form feed at the end of a printout.

File Contents

Options are Text or Byte Stream. Select Byte Stream for all but the most antiquated and "dumb" printers that can only handle strict ASCII characters and can't properly handle the Tab character. In particular, you must select Byte Stream if you will be printing graphics.

Auto Endcap

Select Yes to automatically print your job when you exit an application.

Enable Timeout and Timeout Count

The timeout count, if enabled, establishes the number of seconds of no output to the printer before the system assumes that you are finished printing. At that time, your job will begin to print. If the timeout is used, it is recommended that this be set to a high enough value (approximately 30 seconds) to prevent a job from printing prematurely while your computer is doing something like creating fonts or calculating a graphical output.

You can create a HOLD configuration by selecting no timeout and not selecting Auto endcap. In this case, all printing will be held in the queue until you specifically type **ENDCAP** or set up a new CAPTURE configuration.

Using CAPTURE to Select a Configuration

Once you have defined a print configuration, use the CAPTURE command to begin sending output to a network printer. Use the form **CAPTURE J=<configuration name>** to use a specific print job configuration. Otherwise the default is used. For example, if you had used PRINTCON to set up a HOLD configuration as outlined above, you would use the following command to enable these settings:

```
CAPTURE J=HOLD
```

Using PCONSOLE to Display a Print Queue

The PCONSOLE menu utility provides the easiest way to determine the status of a print queue. The utility allows you to display the jobs that are waiting to be printed. With proper authorization, you can also delete a print job or change its priority. Other features of PCONSOLE are discussed in Unit 17.

Logging Out

End your network session by typing the **LOGOUT** command at the DOS prompt. This will normally leave one network drive (usually drive F:) attached to the LOGIN directory on the server. This will enable you to login again at a later time. Any print jobs that have been sent to the server and are in the queue will still be printed.

Netware 4 Menu Utilities

Most of the above menus carry over to Netware 4 with little change. However, SYSCON has been replaced with a new menu utility, **NETADMIN**, and a new Windows (GUI) application, **NWADMIN**. Both provide the capabilities of SYSCON along with tools to manage Netware Directory Services.

Summary

Netware provides an extensive set of utility menus that can be used to customize and manage the network. These can be accessed by logging into the server and typing **MENU MAIN**, or by typing the name of the specific menu. The menus include SESSION, FILER, VOLINFO, SYSCON, FCONSOLE, PCONSOLE, PRINTCON, and PRINTDEF. From a user's perspective, SYSCON is probably the most important of these for customizing your environment by setting up a login script, while PRINTCON is the most important for setting up your printing.

Review Questions

1. How do you start the Novell main menu?

* 2. Describe the basic functions of each of the eight Novell menus that are accessible through the Novell main menu.

* 3. Describe the purpose of the user login script.

4. How does the use of PRINTCON affect the use of the CAPTURE command?

Exercises

1. Login to your network and use SYSCON to:
   a. Change your password,
   b. Create a login script that sets up a personal drive "I:".
   c. Determine how many user names are defined on your server.

2. Login to your network and determine the number of Netware volumes that are defined, the size of each, and the amount of available storage on each.

3. Login to your network and determine which users are actually logged in to the network. You should be able to do this in two different ways, one through a menu and one through a command.

4. Use the PRINTCON menu to set up two printer configuration files, one called NORMAL and the other called HOLD. The NORMAL configuration should use a timeout of 30 seconds, while HOLD should have no timeout with Auto endcap disabled. Designate NORMAL as the default configuration.

   How do you invoke each of these configurations? Check this by typing **CAPTURE SH** and noting the timeout and Auto endcap settings.

Key Terms

FCONSOLE
FILER
Login Script
LOGOUT
NETADMIN
NWADMIN
PCONSOLE
PRINTCON
PRINTDEF
SESSION
SYSCON
VOLINFO

Unit 13 Introduction to Network Management

As networking becomes more important in an organization, so too does the need for proper operation and management of network resources. Sooner or later, the following management duties and issues will need to be addressed:

➡ Who will be responsible for the installation and maintenance of software? This includes organizing the network hard disk so that all applications are installed in a standard way.

➡ Who will have the authority to decide who gets access to the applications and/or data? Who will implement these decisions? How does this affect security?

➡ Who will be responsible for ensuring integrity of the data stored on the file server, and who will be responsible for creating back-ups? How critical is the data?

➡ What level of knowledge is required for the persons who are responsible for network management tasks? What are the training and support needs?

Learning Objectives

At the completion of this unit, you should be able to

1. list the duties and responsibilities of a network manager,

2. add new users and groups to the network (requires supervisor privilege),

3. understand the use of groups as a network management tool,

4. create a plan for organizing mass storage on the server.

The Network Manager

In a small installation, it is not uncommon for network management responsibilities to be assigned to an internal person who is thoroughly knowledgeable about computers but has other primary duties. In this case, it might be appropriate to hire outside specialists for specific technical tasks. In other situations, management duties may be assigned to one or more full-time computer professionals.

In any case, it is wise to assign specific duties and responsibilities for network management and operation. These might include:

➡ Adding directories to the network drive

➡ Installing and testing network applications software

➡ Adding and deleting usernames and passwords

➡ Assigning access rights to applications and data

➡ Investigating and troubleshooting network problems

➡ Creating backups

➡ Maintaining system security

➡ Providing user support

➡ Monitoring network use

Depending on the circumstances, some of these responsibilities may be more important than others, and additional tasks may need to be added to the list.

A Note on Backups

The importance of making **backup** copies of data will depend on the sensitivity and the amount of data stored on the network. How often backups are made will depend on the importance of the information and the amount and frequency of new data being added to the system. In any case, there should be a backup schedule and a method for rotating tapes so that there is always a set of backups that covers a few weeks of data. In addition, a backup should be set aside at regular intervals, such as at the end of each quarter, should there be a need to recover historical data.

It is also wise to store some of the backups off site or in a fire-proof container.

Adding Users and Groups to the Network

The main SYSCON menu of "Available Topics" is shown in Figure 13-1.

If you select Group Information from the SYSCON Available Topics menu, you will be presented with a list of existing groups. This will include the group EVERYONE, which is always created when you install Netware. Press [Ins] to add a new group or [Enter] to remove a group.

Caution *Do not remove the group EVERYONE. This will alter access rights for all users.*

Figure 13-1
The SYSCON Menu

```
┌─────────────────────────────┐
│     Available Topics        │
├─────────────────────────────┤
│ Accounting                  │
│ Change Current Server       │
│ File Server Information      │
│ Group Information           │
│ Supervisor Options          │
│ User Information            │
│                             │
└─────────────────────────────┘
```

Next, you can highlight one of the listed groups and press Enter. You will see the Group Information menu shown in Figure 13-2. Select Member List on this menu to see a list of users that are members of the group. While viewing the list of members, press Ins or Del to add or remove users from the group.

Figure 13-2
The Group Information Menu

```
┌───────────────────────────┐
│     Group Information      │
├───────────────────────────┤
│ Full Name                 │
│ Member List               │
│ Other Information         │
│ Trustee Assignments       │
└───────────────────────────┘
```

Use the **Trustee Assignments** option to assign trustee privileges that allow group members to access the directories you specify. All of the members of the group inherit the trustee privileges of the group.

If you use Esc to go back to the SYSCON Available Topics menu and select the User Information option, you will see a list of current users. Press Ins to add a new user or Del to remove a user.

When you highlight a user and press Enter you will see the User Information menu shown in Figure 13-3.

Figure 13-3
The User Information Menu

```
┌───────────────────────────┐
│     User Information       │
├───────────────────────────┤
│ Account Restrictions      │
│ Change Password           │
│ Full Name                 │
│ Groups Belonged To        │
│ Login Script              │
│ Other Information         │
│ Security Equivalences     │
│ Station Restrictions      │
│ Time Restrictions         │
│ Trustee Assignments       │
└───────────────────────────┘
```

Selecting User Names

Using Groups as a Management Tool

Many organizations have a standard way to assign all user names. For example, the IBM mail standard specifies the use of the first initial of the first name followed by the first six letters of the last name. A number may be added in the event that more than one user has the same username (JDOE1, JDOE2, and so on).

A Netware **group** allows the network manager to classify users for purposes of granting privileges. In general, the network manager creates a group (such as a company department) and assigns access privileges to the group. Each user in the group then inherits the access privileges.

The group EVERYONE is automatically created when you install Netware, and all new users are automatically included in this group. As a result, the network manager can assign a trustee right to the group EVERYONE and all users inherit its access privileges. For example, if batch files for a menu system have been placed in the SYS:BAT directory, the supervisor can use:

```
GRANT F R SYS:BAT TO GROUP EVERYONE
```

to give EVERYONE File scan (F) and Read (R) access to the BAT directory. As we will discuss in more detail in the next unit, this will allow all users to find and read the batch files, and provides the minimum access privileges required to run the batch files.

Some groups might be related to the applications used on the server. For example, the group 123USERS might include all who need access to the Lotus 1-2-3 program, and the group ACCOUNTING all who need access to the accounting programs.

Other groups, like MARKETING or SALES, might correspond to work groups or departments of your organization. Still others, like DIALIN, might include those who need to be able to dial in to the network from off site.

Generally speaking, it does not hurt to create additional groups if there is a need to distinguish between one subcategory of users and another. A user can be a member of more than one group and inherits access rights from all of them.

Exactly how users are organized into groups is up to each network administrator, but it is well to plan carefully. This will pay off later, when a new user is added or when an existing one needs access to another program or resource. If the groups have been set up properly, the supervisor will only need to add the new user to the appropriate group or groups to provide the necessary access rights. Likewise, if an existing user no longer needs access to a program, he or she can be removed from the corresponding group.

The use of groups also simplifies the network administrator's tasks when a problem is discovered. For example, if you need to change the access rights for a specific program, these changes need to be made only once for the entire group. Each member of the group then inherits the new access rights.

Use GRANT or SYSCON to Assign Trustee Rights

Assign trustee rights to groups through the **GRANT** command, as indicated briefly above, or through the Trustee Assignments part of the Group Information menu or the User Information menu in SYSCON (see Figure 13-3). Detailed meanings of the trustee assignments that can be given to a group are outlined in the next unit.

Organizing the Network Drive

If you are managing a network, it is very important to plan the **directory structure** for the server volume so that applications are installed in a logical and consistent way. For example, you may choose to use a subdirectory of PUBLIC to install files such as DOS utilities to which you want all users to have access. Many network managers will install general-purpose applications in subdirectories of an "applications" directory. (The directory is called APPS in the following example.) Other directories can contain more restricted applications, such as a directory called ADMIN with applications that are available (and of interest) only to a specific group of administrators.

For ease of management, the directory structure and the group structure should go hand-in-hand. The group EVERYONE has access to the PUBLIC directory, and you can also provide Read and Filescan access to directories such as APPS that are to be generally available. It is a good idea to create a Netware GROUP for each class of users that will have exclusive access to a specific application or group of applications. For example, there could be a group called ADMINS with access to applications in the ADMIN directory. In this case, you would assign the group ADMINS the appropriate trustee access rights to the ADMIN directory.

The Directories Created by Netware

When the server is first installed, the following directories are created by Netware:

```
\ ─┬─ LOGIN
   ├─ MAIL
   ├─ PUBLIC
   └─ SYSTEM
```

The LOGIN directory is unique in that it is available to anyone who has attached to the server, even before he or she has logged in. The actual LOGIN program is located there along with any other files that are used before login or after logout. The MAIL directory contains a mail subdirectory for each user. These are used by the system to store files that are unique to each user. The PUBLIC directory contains Netware utilities such as FILER that are generally available to all users. In contrast, the SYSTEM directory contains Netware operating system files that are not required by the average user.

Adding DOS Directories

It is customary to install DOS files on the server and make this directory available to all users. This is especially useful for stations that do not have a local hard disk with DOS files on it. The DOS directories are often installed as subdirectories of PUBLIC. The exact directory structure will depend on the number of different versions of DOS that are being used on your network. The structure shown below assumes that only MS-DOS versions 3.3, 4, and 5 are being used. The appropriate DOS directory can be established as a search drive in the system login script so that all users will have access to the correct DOS files.

Server Volume Example

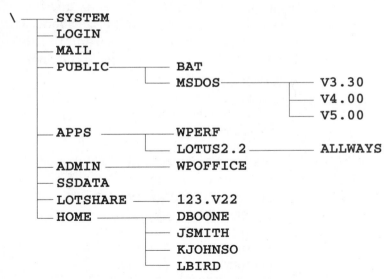

This is a relatively simple structure. Additional directory names might include a shared directory—say, DOCS—for word processing documents that are shared by all users. Instead of a HOME directory with subdirectories for all users, you may wish to create a directory for each workgroup (MARKETING, DEVELOPMENT, and the like) with shared files and subdirectories for each user in that group. The application programs can also be grouped into more specific categories. For example, you may wish to install all utility programs in subdirectories of UTIL, word processing programs in WP, graphics programs in GRAPHICS, spreadsheet programs in SS, and so on. (Note that some network managers prefer to create a USERS directory instead of the HOME directory. The end result is the same, with a subdirectory for each user.)

◆◆
Using LISTDIR to Show a Directory Structure

◆◆
Planning Netware Directory Services (Netware 4.0)

The Netware **LISTDIR** command can be used to display a list of directories and subdirectories on your server. Simply type LISTDIR followed by a network drive letter or a path and the listing will be displayed. (Use NDIR <path> /DO with Netware 4.)

The Netware Directory Services (NDS) provides a new level of flexibility in customizing the network environment. Everything that has been said about planning the hard disk directory structure, and creating users and groups, carries over to the Netware 4 environment. However, with Netware 4, planning is much more global and involves the entire network, not just an individual server.

The NDS includes all network resources such as servers, volumes, groups, printers, and users, as well as organizational units such as divisions or campuses. Furthermore, NDS organizes all these network resources and users into a hierarchical structure. With NDS, a group is seen in the context of a department or division within the organization. Similarly, a departmental printer or a single user is seen within the larger organizational structure. A simple NDS is depicted in the following diagram. In this case, the group LABUSERS is part of the SCIENCE unit as is the printer SPRINT.

```
STATEU (ORG)
├─ADMINS (GROUP)
├─HUMANITIES (ORG UNIT)
│   ├─ BSERV (SERVER)
│   ├─ BSERV_SYS (VOLUME)
│   ├─ WPUSERS (GROUP)
│   └─ AADAMS (USER)
└─SCIENCE (ORG UNIT)
    ├─ NET (SERVER)
    ├─ NET_APPS (VOLUME)
    ├─ NET_SYS (VOLUME)
    ├─ NET_VOL1 (VOLUME)
    ├─ LABUSERS (GROUP)
    ├─ SPRINT (PRINTER)
    └─ JSMITH (USER)
```

The network manager still has complete flexibility to place users in groups, or to organize each network volume into directories and subdirectories. Now, however, the view is network-wide and a group is not specific to a single server. All of this flexibility makes the manager's job much more challenging in the Netware 4 environment.

Summary

The network manager plays an increasingly important role in ensuring the smooth operation of the network, safeguarding data, and providing secure access to network resources. A network manager's duties might include: adding users and groups, organizing the network drives, creating backups, maintaining security, monitoring use, troubleshooting, and providing support.

SYSCON is a versatile utility for assisting the network manager. Among other things, it can be used to add usernames and groups, as well as to assign trustee rights. NETADMIN and NWADMIN are the corresponding utilities in the Netware 4 environment.

Netware creates a standard directory structure that is expanded by the network manager. There is no one set method of creating an expanded network directory structure, but it should be sufficiently well thought out that it makes sense for your environment.

With Netware 4, the Netware Directory Services (NDS) provides a means to organize and manage all resources and users on an entire network. NDS is a flexible and powerful tool that makes the manager's job more complex.

Review Questions

* **1.** What are some of the duties and responsibilities of a typical network manager?

2. Why are backups important?

3. Describe some of the uses of the SYSCON utility.

* **4.** What is the role of the Netware group in assigning access rights?

5. What directories are created when you install Netware?

Exercises

1. Describe the duties and responsibilities of the network manager for your network or for a network with which you are familiar. What are the most important management responsibilities in this environment?

2. Login to your network and use LISTDIR to determine the directory structure. Show the structure using a diagram similar to the one in the text.

3. Login to your network and use SYSCON to determine the groups to which you belong.

Key Terms

Backup

Directory structure

GRANT

Group

LISTDIR

NDIR

Trustee assignment

Unit 14 Providing Access and Maintaining Security

One of the tasks of most network managers is to make the network easy to use and accessible to authorized users, while also maintaining security and guarding against unauthorized access or use. Adequate security is necessary to guard against tampering with data and to ensure that confidential or sensitive data is not seen by those who do not have a "need to know."

Access rights and security restrictions work together to make resources easy to use for authorized personnel while restricting access to others. This unit covers the three main levels of Netware security: general access restrictions, directory access restrictions, and file access restrictions. It also includes a brief discussion of NDS security.

Learning Objectives

At the completion of this unit, you should be able to

1. appreciate the need for network security,
2. understand the levels of Netware access restrictions,
3. determine your access rights in a directory,
4. view the access restrictions for a file.

General Access Restrictions

The Netware operating system, like many others, provides for the creation of user names and passwords. The password provides the initial level of general access restriction. Netware provides a number of access restriction capabilities beyond simple login passwords to help prevent unauthorized access. These include the following restrictions, which can be imposed at the option of the network supervisor:

Account Expiration Date

User accounts can be given an optional expiration date.

Password Requirements

Users can be required to provide a password of a specified length and/or to change the password at specified intervals.

Time Restrictions

A user can be restricted to login only during specified hours on specified days of the week (for example, 8:00 A.M. to 6:00 P.M. Monday through Friday). In addition, Netware 3 and 4 users who log in during the authorized times are forced to logout at the end of the authorized time period.

Intruder Detection/Lockout

When activated, this feature prevents password guessing by allowing only a specified number of attempts to login. If the user is unable to type the correct password within the allotted number of attempts, Netware then locks the account and prevents further logins for a specified length of time.

Station Restrictions

This provides a means to restrict exactly where a given user can log into the network.

These general access restrictions can be used to enhance and strengthen the login password system and can be set for individual users through the SYSCON or NETADMIN utility.

Default Access Restrictions

How the general access restrictions are used will depend on the security needs of each specific network environment. Once policies are set, the network supervisor can set **default access restrictions** using the Supervisor Options menu on the SYSCON utility. The defaults are then set whenever a new user is created. Default access restrictions in Netware 4 are set using a USER-TEMPLATE object associated with an organization or organizational unit.

Directory Access Restrictions

Once the user logs in, Netware imposes access restrictions that govern to which directories or files the user has access and the level of access granted. This type of access is normally granted at the directory level, but can also be set on a file-by-file basis. The net result is that a user cannot view or access the network directory unless that user has been given access to the directory. Additional access rights can be set on a file-by-file basis within a directory. A user can be given access either directly or by being a member of a group that has been given access. Access authorization is called a trustee assignment.

Trustee Assignments

The following "direct" trustee rights can be granted:

C Create and write to new files or subdirectories

E Erase files

F File scan or the ability to see file names

R Read from files

W Write to files

The following "control" rights can also be granted:

A Access Control or the right to grant any of these rights (except S)

M Modify file and directory names, flags, and attributes

S Supervisory; grants all rights in a directory (Netware 3.11 or above only)

Trustee Assignment Examples

The appropriate combination of these rights is required to be able to accomplish a task. Here are some examples:

F is required to see a directory listing with DIR.

R is required to read from a file in the directory.

R and **F** are required to run an executable program.

C is required to create a new subdirectory.

Either **M** or both **C** and **W** are required to rename a file.

W, **C**, **E**, and sometimes **M** are required to write to a closed file.

W, **C**, and **F** are required to copy files to a directory.

R, **W**, **C**, and **F** at the file level (Netware 3.11 and above) and **C** at the directory level are required to recover a deleted file using the SALVAGE utility.

Use the SYSCON utility or the GRANT command to assign trustee rights to a specific user or to a group. (Use NETADMIN with Netware 4.) Use the FILER utility to assign trustee rights for a specific directory or file. For example, the command

```
GRANT F R W FOR SYS:APPS\LOTUS TO JSMITH
```

would be used to give user JSMITH **F**ile scan (**F**), **R**ead (**R**), and **W**rite (**W**) trustee rights in the APPS\LOTUS directory of the SYS: volume.

The TLIST, RIGHTS, and LISTDIR commands can also provide information about access rights in a directory.

The Netware **TLIST** command can be used to view a list of persons or groups granted access to a specific network directory. Type **TLIST** alone to see a list of USERS or GROUPS with access to the current (default) directory, or type **TLIST <path>** to see a list of USERS and GROUPS with access to the specific directory indicated by the **<path>** statement.

The Netware **RIGHTS** command can be used to view your own effective rights in a specific directory. Type **RIGHTS** or **RIGHTS <path>**

to see your effective rights in the current directory or in the specific directory indicated by the **<path>** statement. (See below for additional information about the Netware 4 version of RIGHTS.)

To assign nonsupervisory trustee rights to other users, a user must have the Access Control right. Only supervisors or users with the Supervisory right can assign the Supervisory right to other users.

Guidelines for Assigning Trustee Rights

Appropriate access rights will vary from one application to another. However, there are a few general guidelines:

Use the Minimum Rights Possible. This is a rule akin to "need to know" and helps ensure better network security. For example, R F rights are usually sufficient in, say, the DOS directory where the user only needs to read (in order to run) the programs and utilities located there.

Reserve Rights A M S. These "control" rights are the ones that are potentially most damaging and normally least needed for day-to-day operations.

Inherited Rights Restrictions for a Directory

The supervisor or a user with the **S**upervisory or **A**ccess Control right can specify the maximum trustee rights that can be inherited in a directory. In contrast to the trustee assignments, which are granted to users or groups, the maximum rights restrictions are associated with a directory. With Netware 3, maximum rights restrictions take the form of an **inherited rights mask**, which restricts the trustee access rights that can be inherited from a parent directory whenever an individual is not given specific trustee rights in that directory. This is called the **inherited rights filter** in Netware 4. (With Netware 2.x, this takes the form of a **maximum rights mask**, which restricts the trustee assignments that can be made in the directory. In any case, the default inherited rights restrictions is to allow all rights to be inherited or granted (no maximum rights restrictions).

Use the FILER utility to change the directory rights masks. With Netware 3 you can also use the **ALLOW** command to change an inherited rights mask. For example, use:

```
ALLOW SYS:APPS\LOTUS\DATA TO INHERIT F R
```

to set an inherited rights mask of F R for the APPS\LOTUS\DATA directory. In this case, any user with at least F R rights in the APPS\LOTUS directory will inherit these rights in the APPS\LOTUS\DATA directory. (ALLOW has been incorporated into the RIGHTS command of Netware 4.)

Effective Rights

A user or group can be given explicit rights to a file or directory, or can inherit rights from a parent directory. The net result is called the **effective rights**. With Netware 3 or 4, if a user or group is given explicit rights to a file or directory, then these are the effective rights regardless of any inherited rights restrictions. (In the case of Netware 2, effective rights in a directory are always subject to the restrictions imposed by the maximum rights mask.)

If no rights are explicitly granted to a user in the directory, then the effective rights are the rights inherited from a higher directory, subject to the inherited rights restrictions.

As explained in Unit 13, the Netware **LISTDIR** command is used to display a list of the subdirectories of a given directory. When the /E option is included, LISTDIR also shows your effective rights in each of these directories. To use it, type `LISTDIR /E` or `LISTDIR <path> /E`. (`NDIR <path> /DO` is the equivalent command in Netware 4.)

File and Directory Attributes

The third level of access restriction is normally imposed at the file level, although it can also be set for a directory. The network manager can use file or directory attributes to control access to individual files and can determine how they are used in an application. In contrast to file or directory trustee rights, which are associated with a user or group, file or directory attributes are associated with the file or directory. File attributes are set using the FILER menu or by means of the **FLAG** command.

To set file attributes, a user must have the Modify (M) trustee right in the directory.

Using FLAG to Set File Attributes

The FLAG command can be used to assign or remove file attributes. The most common attributes include:

RO Read-Only (prevents erasure or change)

S Sharable

These attributes can be set using the format

    FLAG F:MYFILE.TXT S RO

The file specification can use wild cards to set the attributes for a group of files. In addition, use the plus or minus sign to add or remove an attribute. For example,

    FLAG *.EXE -RO

would remove the RO attribute from all .EXE files in the current directory. –RO is equivalent to adding the Read-Write attribute (+RW). By default, files are designated to be Read-Write (RW) and do not have the Sharable (S) attribute. This is called the "Normal" attribute and it can be set using the form **FLAG <filename> N**.

FLAG can also be used to mark a file as a **Hidden** file (H) or a **System** file (Sy). Hidden or system files will not appear on a DIR listing and cannot be deleted or copied.

◆ Directory Attributes

Some attributes can be imposed on an entire directory. These include (**H**idden) and (**Sy**stem). These attributes have the same effect: They hide the directory from being listed by DIR, and they prevent it from being deleted or copied. With Netware 3 and above, the FLAGDIR command can be used to set the additional directory attributes of Delete-inhibit, Purge, and Rename-inhibit.

◆ Use *FLAGDIR* to Set Directory Attributes

With Netware 3, you can use the **FLAGDIR** command to set a directory attribute. For example,

    FLAGDIR H

assigns the **H**idden attribute to the current network directory. In this case, the directory will not be shown on a directory listing and cannot be copied. (It will be listed if you use NDIR and have **F**ile scan rights.) With the appropriate access rights, you can still use files that are contained in a hidden directory. **FLAG <path> <attribute> /DO** is the corresponding syntax for Netware 4. Thus, you would type **FLAG . H /DO** to make the current directory a hidden one.

◆ Use of Execute-Only

All versions of Netware allow an executable file to be designated as execute-only using the FILER utility. Once designated as execute-only, a file cannot be copied or modified in any way. This can be a good means of preventing unauthorized copying of program files from the network server. Unfortunately, execute-only files do not always run properly because the program cannot write changes to itself. (WordPerfect is an example of a program that will not run as an execute-only file.)

The process of making a file execute-only is irreversible. Therefore, make sure that you have at least *two* good backups of a file before converting it to execute-only using the **X** attribute. If you need to upgrade or modify the file after it is converted, or want to remove the Execute-Only attribute, your only recourse is to erase the file and restore a backup copy to the network.

◆ File Attributes Available with Netware 3 and 4

Some additional file attributes are available only with Netware 3 and 4. These include:

C   Copy-inhibit

Di Delete-inhibit

P   Purge file when deleted

Ri Rename-inhibit

All of these can be applied on a file-by-file basis, and all but Copy-inhibit can be applied to an entire directory. (In addition, there are some file attributes that are unique to Netware 4 and that relate to its data compression and migration capabilities.)

The **Copy-inhibit** restriction applies only to Macintosh workstations and prevents copying of designated files. **Delete-inhibit** prevents deletion or overwriting of a file or directory. Similarly, **Rename-inhibit** prevents renaming of a file or directory. The Delete-inhibit and Rename-inhibit attributes are automatically set whenever a file is made "Read-Only." The **Purge** attribute prevents a deleted file or directory from being salvaged.

File Attributes Override Trustee Assignments

File (and directory) attributes, when set, will override trustee assignments. For example, a supervisor or a user having the Erase trustee right in a directory will not be able to erase a file that has been made **R**ead-**O**nly. To erase the file, its RO access restriction must first be changed to **R**ead-**W**rite.

Netware 4 Management Tools

Many of the management utilities have been revised and improved with Netware 4. Some utilities have been retained, while others have been expanded or replaced with other tools. Some of the most important changes have already been mentioned. The most significant change is a new Windows-based GUI tool called NWADMIN that is both powerful and intuitive. This, together with NETADMIN (its text-based DOS counterpart), replaces SYSCON. (Netware 4 also includes a GUI utility called NWUSER that users can run from within Windows to accomplish tasks such as setting up a drive mapping, or connecting to a printer.)

Other commands have been consolidated. For example, GRANT, ALLOW, and TLIST have been eliminated in favor of a more powerful RIGHTS command. Here is a brief summary of these changes:

Use `RIGHTS <path> <attributes> /Name=<username>` instead of `GRANT`.

Use `RIGHTS <path> <mask> /F` instead of `ALLOW`.

Use `RIGHTS <path> /T` instead of `TLIST`.

Netware 4 also features on-line documentation and more extensive help. For example, you can type `RIGHTS /?` to get Netware help for the RIGHTS command.

Netware 4 NDS Security

The Netware Directory Services incorporates another layer of security. In particular, the network administrator uses the NWADMIN or NETADMIN utilities to allow access to objects such as printers, file servers, or volumes in the NDS structure. This access must be granted in addition to the access rights that have been discussed for Netware 2 and 3. This makes the network manager's job considerably more complicated with Netware 4. However, once the environment has been properly set up, the user will be able to take advantage of an intuitive, easy-to-use view of network resources.

Summary

Netware provides three levels of security: password and related security measures provide general access restrictions; trustee assignments provide access to directories or files; and attributes restrict activities that can be performed with a file or directory.

Before users can enter the network, they must be given a user account (usually with a password) and must be given trustee assignments to network directories or files. Attribute restrictions apply to all users.

Netware includes a versatile and flexible set of tools to manage access to resources. The most useful is the SYSCON menu utility, which allows the network manager to customize password security and make trustee assignments. The FILER utility can be used to set trustee assignments and attributes. The Netware commands GRANT, ALLOW, FLAG, and FLAGDIR can also be used to accomplish many of the same tasks. NWADMIN, NETADMIN, RIGHTS and FLAG are the primary management tools for Netware 4, replacing SYSCON, ALLOW, GRANT, LISTDIR, and TLIST.

These tools allow the network manager to create a secure environment where authorized users can have easy access to the data and programs they need.

Review Questions

* 1. What are the (login) access restrictions that would apply to most Novell networks?

2. List the eight trustee assignments that are possible with Netware. Which three are generally reserved?

* 3. What are the two most commonly used file attributes?

* 4. If a Netware version 3 or 4 user is given specific trustee rights, what are the effective rights?

Exercises

1. Use the User Information menu in the SYSCON utility (or NETADMIN) to select your username and determine the values of the following restrictions for your network account:

   a. Password requirements

   b. Time restrictions

   c. Intruder detection/lockout status

2. Determine your effective rights in the SYS:SYSTEM directory and the SYS:PUBLIC directory. Do these make sense?

3. Login to your network.

   a. Make your own directory the default (that is, go to a directory such as USERS/JSMITH where you are user JSMITH and have been given trustee rights in this directory).

   b. Use the RIGHTS command to verify your trustee rights in the directory.

   c. Use the FLAG command to view the attributes of a file in the directory. Use the FLAG command to change the file attribute to RO. Were you allowed to do this? Why?

   d. Next, make a copy of the file using COPY and attempt to erase the file using the ERASE command. What is the message that is returned? Can you erase the copy? Why?

4. User SAM is given rights using the following GRANT statement:

   GRANT C E F R W FOR SYS:APPS\LOTUS TO USER SAM

   There are no directory access restrictions in SYS:APPS\LOTUS, but the supervisor has imposed an inherited rights mask (or maximum rights mask) in SYS:APPS\LOTUS\DATA using

   ALLOW SYS:APPS\LOTUS\DATA TO INHERIT F R

   What are SAM's effective rights in SYS:APPS\LOTUS and in SYS:APPS\LOTUS\DATA?

Key Terms and Commands

Access Control (Trustee right)

ALLOW

Copy-inhibit (File attribute)

Create (Trustee right)

Default access restrictions

Delete-inhibit (Directory/file attribute)

Effective rights

Erase (Trustee right)

EXecute-Only (File attribute)

File scan (Trustee right)

FLAG

FLAGDIR

Hidden (Directory/file attribute)

Inherited rights filter

Inherited rights mask

LISTDIR /E

Maximum rights mask

Modify (Trustee right)

Purge (Directory/file attribute)

Read (Trustee right)

Read **O**nly (File attribute)

Rename-**i**nhibit (Directory/file attribute)

RIGHTS

Sharable (File attribute)

Supervisory (Trustee right)

System (Directory/file attribute)

TLIST

Write (Trustee right)

Unit 15 Using Login Scripts

This unit shows how the login script can be used to customize the Netware environment much like the AUTOEXEC.BAT file can be used to customize the DOS environment.

Learning Objectives

At the completion of this unit, you should be able to

1. list the kinds of Netware login scripts,
2. understand the use of the system login script,
3. customize your user login script.

Types of Login Scripts

There are three kinds of Netware login scripts: the system login script, the user login script, and the default login script. If there is a system login script, it is executed first. Normally, the network manager will define a system login script that sets up the environment for all users. An example of a system login script is given in a later section. If there is one, the user login script is invoked next. A user login script contains commands that customize the Netware environment for an individual user. The user can add or remove lines from this script. (This is in contrast to the system login script where only the supervisor can make changes.) Finally, the default login script is invoked if there is no user script defined.

A login script can be used for a number of things. These include: setting up a network drive, attaching a station to additional servers, setting up printers, checking for security problems, or starting a menu application.

Default Login Script

The **default login script** is coded into the netware operating system and cannot be modified. It is not executed if there is a user login script defined (even if the user login script contains only a single remark line). It does, however, contain a number of examples of how a login script can be used. Its (effective) content is as shown below:

```
WRITE "Good %GREETING_TIME, %LOGIN_NAME."
MAP DISPLAY OFF
MAP ERRORS OFF
MAP *1:=SYS:
MAP *1:=SYS:%LOGIN_NAME
IF "%1"="SUPERVISOR" THEN MAP *1:=SYS:SYSTEM
MAP S1:=SYS:PUBLIC
MAP S2:=S1:%MACHINE/%OS/%OS_VERSION
MAP DISPLAY ON
MAP
```

The following notes and comments explain the workings of the default login script:

➡ The first line uses the system variables **%GREETING_TIME**, which evaluates to morning, afternoon, or evening, depending on the time of day, and **%LOGIN_NAME**, which evaluates to the user's login name. Thus, if JSMITH is logging in at 9:00 A.M., this line displays the greeting: "Good morning, JSMITH."

➡ ***1:** refers to the first available network drive letter. This is usually drive F:.

➡ A repeated drive mapping overwrites the previous MAP statement unless the system cannot carry out the command. Thus, if JSMITH is logging in and there is no SYS:JSMITH directory, then F:=SYS:. If there is a JSMITH directory, then F:=SYS:JSMITH, because **MAP *1:=SYS:%LOGIN_NAME** overwrites the previous map assignment.

➡ The default value of **%MACHINE** is IBMPC. This can be changed using a NET.CFG or SHELL.CFG file at the workstation.

➡ The value of **%OS** is MSDOS for a machine running the DOS operating system.

➡ In the case of an MS-DOS machine, the value of **%OS_VERSION** depends on the version of DOS being used. The use of **%OS_VER-SION** will be illustrated in more detail below.

System Login Script

The **system login script** is useful in setting up resources that might be required by all users. For example, all of the network's users will need to have a search drive mapped to the PUBLIC directory in order to have access to Netware system resources.

Identifier Variables

Identifier variables such as %LOGIN_NAME can be used in the system login script to set up customized mappings or to carry out conditional statements. For example, the line `MAP *1:=SYS:` `%LOGIN_NAME` will set up a custom mapping to a directory that has the same name as the user's login name.

Other identifier variables such as `%OS` and `%OS_VERSION` can be used to establish drive mappings to the directory on the server containing the DOS files that are appropriate for the user.

Conditional Statements in a Login Script

Conditional statements in a login script allow additional flexibility to carry out statements for specific users or groups. For example, the line `IF MEMBER_OF "groupname"` will carry out specific login script commands *only* if the user is a member of the named group "groupname."

Login Script Example

Here is an example of some of the commands that can be included in a system login script. This example assumes the following:

➡ The network administrator has created specific directories for each version of DOS. In particular, DOS 3.3 files should be installed on the network in a directory called \PUBLIC\MSDOS\ V3.30, while DOS 5 files should be installed in a directory called \PUBLIC\MSDOS\V5.00. The line

    MAP INS S3:=SYS:\PUBLIC\%OS\%OS_VERSION

creates a search mapping to the directory that corresponds to the version of DOS being used at login. (The Novell variables `%OS` and `%OS_VERSION` evaluate to MS-DOS and a string like V3.30, V4.00, or V5.00 respectively, depending on the DOS version in use at login.)

➡ The network administrator has created the group 123USERS. This is used in the section that begins with `IF MEMBER OF "123USERS"` to set up mappings required by the Lotus 1-2-3 program.

➡ The network administrator has created the appropriate "home" directory for each user. In this example, if there is a user name JSMITH, there should be a directory called \HOME\JSMITH. This is used in the line

    MAP I:=SYS:\HOME\%LOGIN_NAME

to associate the drive letter I: with the user's "personal" directory. In this case, when JSMITH logs in, the macro `%LOGIN_NAME` evaluates to JSMITH.

This also assumes that the network administrator has set up user menus in the AUTOMENU directory, and that these user menus are initiated using a batch file AUTO.BAT. In particular, the last three lines set up a mapping for drive N:, make this the default, and begin the AUTO.BAT file just after exiting from the login script.

```
MAP INS S1:=SYS:PUBLIC
MAP INS S2:=SYS:AUTOMENU
MAP INS S3:=SYS:PUBLIC\%OS\%OS_VERSION
IF MEMBER OF "123USERS" THEN BEGIN
    MAP INS S5:=SYS:HOME\%LOGIN_NAME
    MAP L:=SYS:APPS\LOTUS
END
MAP I:=SYS:HOME\%LOGIN_NAME
SET PROMPT="$P$G"
MAP N:=SYS:AUTOMENU
DRIVE N:
EXIT "AUTO"
```

Here is a brief description of what these lines accomplish:

➡ **MAP INS** inserts a new drive mapping without deleting any previous mappings that might have been set (for example by the DOS PATH command).

➡ The block of commands from the **BEGIN** to the **END** is carried out if the user is a member of the group called 123USERS.

➡ The **SET PROMPT** command sets the DOS prompt.

➡ The **DRIVE** command sets drive N: as the default drive.

➡ The **EXIT** command exits to the batch file AUTO.BAT.

➡ The use of **EXIT** bypasses any user login script that might have been defined.

➡ Many network managers use the EXIT command as shown to bypass the user login script. If you want to use EXIT to load a memory-resident program, but do not wish to bypass the user login script, place the appropriate EXIT command at the end of each user login script. (However, this is usually not the optimum way to manage a network because it creates more work for the network manager.)

Caution   *Never load memory-resident programs from within a login script. This gobbles up system memory by leaving a "hole" in memory that cannot be used. Instead, use a DOS batch file to load the memory-resident program and EXIT to the batch file as in the example.*

User Login Script

You can use the SYSCON utility to access your personal **user login script**. Type **SYSCON** and select User Information. Then select your own user name from the list and Login Script from the next menu. You can then edit your login script.

Note   *You will not be able to edit your login script if the supervisor has disabled the capability to set your own password.*

Unless you have supervisor privileges, you will only be able to modify your own login script. If you have supervisor privileges, you can access any user's login script using the same procedure and can also access the system login script under Supervisor Options. A login script can also be used to set up a default printer or to customize the DOS environment. For example, the command SET PROMPT="PG" can be used to set the DOS prompt.

Additional Features of Netware 4

With Netware 4, a container login script associated with an organization or organizational unit serves as a system login script. Thus, each organization or division can have its own system login script. In addition, the system administrator can define a profile object and an associated login script. Any user can be associated with a profile, much like any user can be associated with a group.

When a Netware 4 user logs in, first the system login script associated with the user's home container executes. Next, a **profile login script** executes if appropriate, and then the user's login script executes. Otherwise, the login scripts function in much the same way as in the Netware 2 and 3 environment.

Summary

The login script offers a powerful and flexible way to customize the Netware environment for each user. The system manager should use the system login script whenever possible to set up a consistent user environment.

Review Questions

1. What are the types of login scripts?
* 2. When is the default login script executed?
* 3. What does the "%" in a login script WRITE statement mean?
* 4. Describe how the IF statement can be used within a login script.

Exercises

1. Use SYSCON/User Information/Login Script (or the NETADMIN utility) to create a user login script for yourself. Set up a drive mapping I: that points to your own home directory.
2. Use the Netware help utility to determine the variables such as LOGIN_NAME that can be used in a login script.
3. Use the line "FIRE PHASERS 5 TIMES" in a login script. What happens when you log in?

Key Terms

System login script
Default login script
Profile login script
User login script

Unit 16 **Installing a Typical Application**

The installation of new applications on the network is an important activity, done primarily by the network manager. This section outlines some of the steps involved in this process. At the same time, the discussion serves to bring together several concepts discussed earlier.

Learning Objectives

At the completion of this unit, you should be able to

1. understand the steps required to install a typical application,

2. see the relation between the creation of a new directory, the setting of a trustee assignment, and the use of MAP statements in the login script,

3. appreciate how file attributes are used in a typical network situation.

General Procedure

Installation of a network-specific version of a software package is usually a matter of following the instructions. However, there are often other considerations, such as access rights, that are not always spelled out in the documentation. The general procedure for installing an application usually starts with the following steps:

➡ Login as SUPERVISOR.

➡ Create a directory for the application.

➡ MAP a logical drive to the directory.

➡ Copy or install the application to the directory.

➡ FLAG all program files as read-only (RO).

In some cases, the installation program will automate much of this process.

Providing Access

Next, the network manager will need to provide the appropriate users or GROUPS with access (trustee rights) to the directory that contains the application. In most cases, it is best to assign the trustee rights to a group. You may wish to create a new group for this purpose. In many cases **F**ile scan and **R**ead access are enough, while other programs will require that the user have one or more of the **W**rite, **C**reate, **E**rase, and **M**odify rights in the program directory in order to run properly. In addition, the system login script may need to be modified to ensure that search mappings or logical drives are set up correctly.

Making It Easy to Start the Application

Once an application has been installed and the appropriate users and user groups have been given access, the network manager will need to provide an easy way to start the application. In some cases, the directory with the application in it can be put on a search path so that the application can be started by typing the appropriate command. However, this does not work with every application and does not give the network manager control over the network environment when the application starts.

Many network administrators prefer to use a menu system to provide access to applications. This can make it easy for the user to run standard applications such as word processing and gives the network administrator more control over setting up printers, mapping paths to data directories, and organizing other elements of the Netware environment. There are many menu systems that can be used, including the Novell menu system, a commercial program such as WordPerfect Office, a shareware program, or a system of batch files. In any case, one important goal of a good network administrator is to make the network as "transparent" as possible so as not to get in the way of the user.

Testing the Setup

Finally, the network administrator should create a new, fictitious user, make that user a member of the group associated with the application, login as that user, and thoroughly test the new software. This "debugging" is important in ensuring that there will be fewer problems when real users start calling upon the new application.

Using the Novell Menu System

Novell includes a menu maker that can be used to create custom menus for your environment. The menu program is included with Netware 2 and 3. You create your own menus by using an editor and setting up menu definition files with a specific format. Note the following:

➡ Menu title lines begin with %

➡ Menu choices or options are lines that start in column 0

➡ Menu actions are indented below the option.

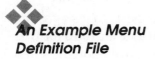

An Example Menu Definition File

The following menu definition file creates a menu with 2 lines. Each of these lines leads to another menu. The second menu carries out the tasks.

```
%Sample Menu Using the Novel Menu Program
1. Network User Information
   %Net Info
2. Network Utilities
   %Netutils


%Net Info
List current network users
   userlist /a
   pause
Show information about yourself
   whoami /a
   pause


%Netutils
File Maintenance Utility
   FILER
System Configuration Utility
   SYSCON
Print Queue Maintenance
   PCONSOLE
```

Once you have created a menu definition file, save it using a file name of the form MYMENU.MNU where MYMENU can be any name you want. The menu definition file should be located in a directory where the user has **R**ead, **W**rite, **C**reate and **E**rase rights. The MENU program itself is in the PUBLIC directory, which should always have a search drive mapped to it. To run the menu program, make the directory containing the menu definition file the default directory, and type the command MENU MYMENU. The Novell menu program will do the rest.

The Novell menu program uses a significant amount of RAM (more than 100KB) and, therefore, may not be appropriate for some applications. The newer NMENU program, included with Netware 4, should be used if available because it requires less system memory.

The NMENU Program

The **NMENU** program, provided with Netware 4, produces menus that are similar in function and appearance to the MENU program. However, NMENU has more features, uses only 32KB of memory in normal operation and requires no memory when running applications in batch mode.

As with the MENU program, you can use any text editor to create a menu definition file. In addition, Netware 4 provides the MENUCNVT program to convert programs from the MENU format to the NMENU format.

Installation Example

The following is an outline of the process that might be used to install the network pack for Lotus 1-2-3. It provides a good example of a network-specific software package that is relatively complex to set up. It is installed in several stages:

Login as SUPERVISOR.

Create directories for the application.

In this case, the network manager chooses to install the application files in the directory \APPS\LOTUS. The accompanying add-in program, called WYSIWYG (what you see is what you get), is installed in \APPS\LOTUS\ADDINS. Lotus uses a directory called LOTSHARE\ 123.V23 to store files that count the number of valid users, so this must also be created. In addition, Lotus stores setup and configuration files in a personal directory, so the network manager will use the \HOME\<login_name> directory for each user. Finally, for the convenience of users, the network manager sets up a directory called SSDATA to contain shared files to which all users have access.

MAP a logical drive to the lotus directory.

In this case, drive L: (for Lotus) has not been used, so the network manager will use this letter. The following line is typed at the console and inserted into the system login script:

```
MAP L:=SYS:APPS\LOTUS
```

Install the program.

This involves copying the files or running the install program. Once files have been copied, the administrator sets the License Count to indicate the number of licensed copies available. This is done using the COUNT program from the LOTUS directory. This same program can be used to view the log file (to determine how many users were denied access to LOTUS) as well as to erase the log file.

FLAG the appropriate files.

In this case, the program files are flagged RO.

Establish a user group and specify trustee rights.

In this case, the network manager creates a group called 123USERS and provides trustee rights as follows:

APPS\LOTUS	File scan **R**ead
LOTSHARE\123.V22	File scan **R**ead **C**reate **E**rase **M**odify **W**rite
SSDATA	File scan **R**ead **C**reate **E**rase **M**odify **W**rite

Of course, each user should have already been provided full access to the personal directory

```
USERS\<username>
```

Modify the system login script.

The appropriate mappings are set up so that Lotus can find the configuration file for each user and to set up user access to personal directories. Here is an example of how this can be done:

```
IF MEMBER OF "123USERS" THEN BEGIN
    MAP INS S5:=SYS:HOME\%LOGIN_NAME
    MAP J:=SYS:HOME\%LOGIN_NAME
    MAP L:=SYS:APPS\LOTUS
END
```

In this case, if user JOE is a member of the group 123USERS, then this sets up the directory HOME\JOE as both a search directory and as drive J:, and sets up the LOTUS program directory as logical drive L:.

Use the NEWUSER program to set up the user directory.

The NEWUSER program is provided with the LOTUS LAN pack and is used to set up the appropriate files in the user's personal directory. Usage is:

```
NEWUSER J:USERS\JOE
```

Automate the startup of the program.

Create a batch file, or modify your menu program, to start Lotus. The exact commands you need would depend on your network environment. For example, if all users will be printing to a single shared printer, then LPT1: should be captured to the network printer as part of the program startup.

Run the Lotus install program.

Each user may need to run the Lotus install program to customize his or her Lotus setup. The install program modifies the user's personal copy of the Lotus 123.SET file to conform to the individual hardware environment. If the hardware environments are identical, the 123.SET file can be copied to the individual user directories.

Test the setup.

Create a new user, say 123USER, then put the user into the group 123USERS and test the setup. It is especially important to test printing to ensure that Lotus and the network have been set up properly. For example, the hardware setup in Lotus should specify a printer on Device LPT1:, not parallel port 1. The latter designation is the default for a local printer, but will not work properly with a network printer.

Summary

The installation of a typical network application can involve a number of steps and illustrates several of the concepts we have discussed. The process may include the following:

→ Logging in as SUPERVISOR

→ Creating a directory for the application

→ Installing the application or copying the appropriate files

→ Creating a GROUP

→ Granting a trustee assignment

→ Modifying the system login script

→ Creating or modifying a menu or batch file to start the application

→ Testing the installation as a typical user

Review Questions

1. In the Lotus example, which trustee rights are granted to the members of the 123USERS group for each directory? Would a user in the 123USERS group be able to edit a file stored in SSDATA? Would the user be able to erase a file in SSDATA?

* 2. The supervisor has installed Lotus, as indicated in the example, and would like to place sample spreadsheet templates in the SSDATA directory. The supervisor does not want users to change the templates. How could the sample files be protected against deletion or editing?

3. After the Lotus files are installed, the supervisor logs in as 123USER and tests the setup. Why not test it as user SUPERVISOR?

Exercises

1. Pick an application on your network and determine the steps taken to install it.

2. Create a menu definition file that is able to launch the applications programs that you use most often. These might include a word processor, a spreadsheet program, and a game. Save the menu definition file to your personal (HOME or USER) directory.

3. Modify the menu of exercise 2 to include the additional option "Printer Setup." This selection should call a submenu with the following options:

Connect to a network printer

Connect to local printer

Display printer connections

Set up/change print configurations

Save the revised menu definition to your home directory.

Key Terms

MENU

MENUCNVT

NMENU

Unit 17 **Managing Network Printing**

Netware printing, when properly installed, is relatively easy to use. However, it can be rather tricky to set up. This section covers the most important aspects of setting up printing on a Novell network.

Learning Objectives

At the completion of this unit, you should be able to

1. understand the process used to print a document on the network,
2. list the types of print services available on a Novell network,
3. understand the relation between a print queue and a printer,
4. outline the steps required to set up printing on a Novell network,
5. use PRINTCON and PRINTDEF to set up a print queue and define special forms and modes,
6. modify the AUTOEXEC.NCF file to automatically start a print server.

Printing Overview

From the the user's perspective, a typical print job begins at the workstation, is redirected by the network software to the appropriate print queue, and is then printed on a network printer, as depicted in Figure 17-1. The network software may also add setup codes for the printer and attach a header sheet that identifies to whom the printed output belongs.

Some network-specific software will interact directly with a print queue. In this case, the software takes care of directing print jobs to the network queue. Other applications must be "tricked" to print to a network printer. In this case, the CAPTURE command is used to redirect output from the local printer port to the network printer. The application software need not be modified. It sends output to the local printer port while the network software takes care of rerouting it first to the network print queue and then to a printer.

The Netware Print Server

The Netware **print server** is an important addition to Netware 3.x and can also be used with Netware 2.2 and above. The print server provides a flexible and controlled way to share printers anywhere on a network by queuing up jobs and parceling them out one at a time to a printer. Netware 2 provides printing services as part of the core operating system, but limits them to five printers attached directly to the server.

Figure 17-1
Printing Overview

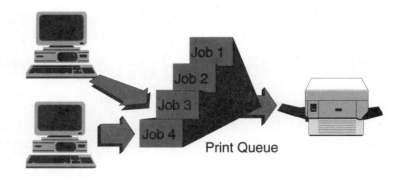

The overview and diagram in Figure 17-1 is typical of Netware 2 core printing. The diagram in Figure 17-2 illustrates the role of the Netware print server, which acts as a "traffic cop" between print queues and printers.

Figure 17-2
The Print Server

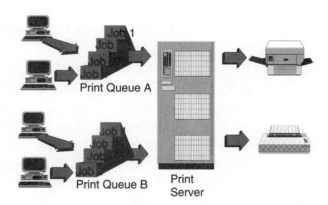

The Netware print server provides a flexible way to set up printing services. A print server can service any number of queues and up to 16 printers (256 for Netware 4) can be located either at a print server or at a remote nondedicated workstation.

In addition, print servers can perform sophisticated printer management tasks. For example, if there is a printer problem, a print server can send a notification to one or more designated network administrators or users.

Planning Print Services

With the flexibility of the print server and the availability of Netware core printing, there are many ways that print services can be set up.

Core Printing

Core printing is only available on Netware 2 and provides the easiest way to set up print services. Network printers are attached directly to the serial or parallel ports of the file server, as shown in Figure 17-3.

Figure 17-3
Core Printing

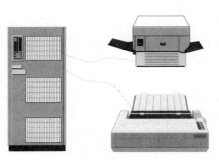

Up to 5 printers can be
connected to the file server

If your network uses Netware 2 and only needs a few printers located at the file server, then core printing will be the quickest to set up and use.

Print Server

All versions of Netware 2.2 and higher can be set up to use a print server. The print server can either be loaded on a file server or run at a dedicated workstation. (Netware 4.0 does not support a dedicated print server.) In either configuration, you can connect printers directly to the print server, and can also connect remote printers, as explained below. When loaded on a file server, a print server has a layout that looks much like core printing.

Print Server at a Dedicated Workstation

The primary advantage of using a dedicated print server is that it can be located anywhere on the network, as depicted in Figure 17-4. This allows a more secure configuration because the file server can be located in a protected area while the print server can be set up where it is most convenient. In addition, the print server offloads

Figure 17-4
Dedicated Print
Server

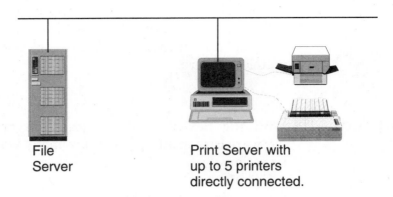

File
Server

Print Server with
up to 5 printers
directly connected.

some of the server workload associated with sending output to the
printers.

The primary disadvantage of using a dedicated print server is that it
requires that a workstation be devoted to this task. However, a print
server does not place great demands on a system, so an older PC is
an acceptable candidate.

Remote Printers

In planning print services, you may wish to share specific printers
on the network and still use the computer to which they are attached
as a network workstation. This type of printer setup is called a
remote printer and is illustrated in Figure 17-5.

Using the **RPRINTER** program (**NPRINTER** for Netware 4), the
network administrator can convert a "private" printer anywhere on
the network into a shared network printer. Remote printers operate
in conjunction with a print server located on the same network.

Figure 17-5
Remote Printer

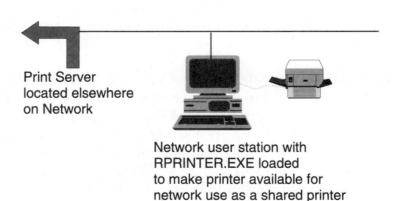

Print Server
located elsewhere
on Network

Network user station with
RPRINTER.EXE loaded
to make printer available for
network use as a shared printer

Setting Up Print Queues

Print queues are used by all forms of Netware print services. The print queue handles the tasks of storing the output as it is being sent from the user's application, and then sending it to the appropriate print server and printer.

The network supervisor can control who has access to use a print queue and who can manage the queue. By default, the group EVERY-ONE can use a print queue and SUPERVISOR can manage the queue as the print **queue operator**. However, the SUPERVISOR can designate other users or groups as print queue operators, and can also designate a more restricted group of **queue users**.

The network SUPERVISOR can use the PCONSOLE menu utility to create print queues. Normally, one print queue is created for each printer and the queue is given a name that is descriptive of the associated printer. However, there is no fixed association between a queue and a printer.

Queues are logically associated with a printer, usually through the print server. The SUPERVISOR configures each network printer to receive its input from one or more print queues. This is normally done by using the PCONSOLE utility when a print server is created or configured (or by using the PRINTER command at the server console for Netware 2 core printing).

The association between a queue and a printer is quite flexible. For example, two queues can send output to the same printer. In this case, the printer will accept a print job from whichever queue has one ready to print. If the queues have been set up with different priorities, jobs in the higher priority queue (lower priority number) will always print before jobs in the other one. Alternatively, two or more printers can be used to serve the same queue. This might be done in a situation where the queue has too much activity for one printer. In this case, a print job would be printed on the first available printer serving the queue.

Setting Up Core Printing

Setting up Netware core printing is generally a four-step process:

1. Connect the printers.
2. Create print queues.
3. Define the printers.
4. Associate queues with printers.

Netware 2 core printing is configured at the server console. First, attach the printers to the server's parallel or serial ports. Once the printers have been connected, you can use the :QUEUE console command to list the print queues that have been defined. You may also use the form :QUEUE <name> CREATE to create print queues, (Print queues can also be created by the SUPERVISOR using the PCONSOLE utility.) For example, you can create a queue called HPLASER using the command

```
QUEUE HPLASER CREATE
```

Next use the :PRINTER command to list the printers that have been defined. You may use the form :PRINTER <#> CREATE <port> to define a printer and the interface (port) to which it is attached. Once the printer has been defined, use the form :PRINTER <#> ADD QUEUE <qname> to define the queue that will send its output to that printer.

For example, assume you have connected an HP LaserJet to the LPT1: port on the server. You can define the printer and connect it to the queue using the following console commands:

```
PRINTER 1 CREATE LPT1
PRINTER 1 ADD QUEUE HPLASER
```

Note *The words PRINTER and QUEUE in the above commands can be abbreviated to P and Q respectively.*

❖
Automating the Printer Setup for Netware 2 Core Printing

Unfortunately, some of the setup for Netware core printing may be lost when you shut down the file server and start it up again. To avoid the need for setting up printing each time you restart the server, place the printer setup commands in the Netware AUTO-EXEC.SYS file. Netware 2 uses this file much like the DOS AUTO-EXEC.BAT file to automate the process of setting up the server when it is powered up. This file most often is used to set up printers, and might contain the two PRINTER commands in the previous example. As another example, consider the following situation:

➥ A LaserJet printer is attached to the parallel port LPT1:.

➥ A serial printer is attached to the serial port COM1: and uses the Netware default communication parameters (9600 baud, 8 data bits, 1 stop bit, no parity).

➥ There are three print queues defined: HPLASER, PRINTQ_0, and PRINTQ_1.

In this case, the following lines might appear in the system AUTO-EXEC file to set up the printers:

```
PRINTER 0 CREATE COM1
PRINTER 0 ADD QUEUE PRINTQ_0
PRINTER 1 CREATE LPT1
PRINTER 1 ADD QUEUE PRINTQ_1
PRINTER 1 ADD QUEUE HPLASER
```

Print queue commands need not be placed in the AUTOEXEC.SYS file because the print queues, once set up, remain on the server and do not need to be created again.

Setting Up a Print Server

Setting up a print server is generally a seven-step process:

1. Connect the printers.
2. Create print queues.
3. Create a print server.
4. Define the printers.
5. Associate queues with printers.
6. Start the print server.
7. Set up remote printers.

Setting Up and Configuring Printers

As mentioned earlier, the print server can be located on the file server or on a dedicated workstation. Once you have decided on the location of the print server and the printers, the printers should be connected. This is relatively straightforward, except possibly for printers that use a serial interface. In this case, a special cable may be required and the print server should be set up to use the same serial communications parameters as the printer.

Setting Up Queues and the Print Server

Next, use PCONSOLE to create print queues. Since a queue is the entity that the user sees, choose a name that is short yet descriptive of the printer to be used with it. For example, you may wish to use ACTG_LJIII if the queue will send its output to the LaserJet III in the Accounting Department, or APPLE for an Applewriter print queue.

Use PCONSOLE to create and configure the print server. If there is more than one print server on your network, it is a good idea to choose a name for the print server that corresponds to the group being serviced. This name will also be used when you start the **PSERVER** program (or NLM).

You define printers and associate each with a queue as part of the print server configuration process. Again, use PCONSOLE to define the printers. Each is given a name and associated with a specific serial or parallel port on the print server or a remote workstation. Any special communication parameters can be specified at this time.

Finally, each defined printer is associated with one or more print queues. Here is where the ACTG_LJIII queue might be associated with the printer attached to the first parallel port of the print server (presumably a LaserJet III in the Accounting Department).

Starting the Print Server

Once you have defined the print server, it will need to be started. The programs you need to install and use depend on which configuration you are using and the location of the print server:

Location of Print Server	Program
At Netware 2.2 server	PSERVER.VAP
At Netware 3.x or 4.x server	PSERVER.NLM
At dedicated workstation	PSERVER.EXE

A print server is normally set up to start when the host system is started. If you are using a dedicated print server, you can copy PSERVER.EXE and supporting files to the boot disk, then create an AUTOEXEC.BAT and a NET.CFG file. The AUTOEXEC.BAT file should contain commands to load the network shell and PSERVER. The NET.CFG file should contain the line **SPX connections=60**. If you are using Netware 2, ensure that PSERVER.VAP is in the SYSTEM directory of the server and restart the system to load the VAP. If you are using a print server on a Netware 3 or 4 file server, you can use the :LOAD PSERVER <name> and :UNLOAD PSERVER <name> console commands to start and stop the print server. In this case, the LOAD PSERVER <name> command can be included in the AUTOEXEC.NCF file to automatically load the print server every time the server is started.

You will also need to load RPRINTER.EXE (or NPRINTER.EXE) at each workstation that has a remote printer attached. This is a TSR (terminate and stay resident) program that uses about 7KB of memory. It is a good idea to create an AUTOEXEC.BAT file at the workstation to load the program whenever the system is turned on. Use the format RPRINTER <print server name> <printer number> to connect the remote printer to the print server. For example, the AUTOEXEC.BAT file might include:

```
IPX
NETX
LOGIN GUEST
RPRINTER WILLOW 3
LOGOUT
CLS
ECHO Printer has been set up for network use
LOGIN
```

The corresponding NPRINTER syntax is:

```
NPRINTER <print server name> <printer name>
```

Note that only an active connection to the file server is required for the remote printer to function properly. The printer can be shared even if no user is logged in at the workstation.

Customizing Print Services

Once print services have been set up, network users can use the CAPTURE command to redirect output to the print queue. As indicated in Unit 11, the PRINTCON utility can be used to create custom printing configurations.

In addition, printing can be customized by using special **forms** as well as controlled through the use of **print commands** that are sent to the printer before each print job. This can be useful for resetting the printer before each print job or for setting up special typefaces, margin settings, or form lengths. Netware further refines this by grouping multiple commands into a **mode** setup. The use of print devices, modes, and forms is described below.

Print Devices and Modes

The **PRINTDEF** utility is the primary tool for setting up print **devices** and modes.

Print Devices

A print device refers to both a given printer, such as a LaserJet II, and a collection of functions and modes that apply to operations on that printer. Several print device definitions exist in the PUBLIC directory of the Netware server. There are approximately 35 print devices predefined and, in most cases, the network manager can simply import the appropriate file. To do so, start PRINTDEF and choose the Import Print Device option.

Print Device Functions

Print **functions** are special operations that can be used to program or configure the printer. Each function corresponds to a command code that can be sent to the printer as part of a print job. The command code is interpreted by the printer as a nonprinting command. Typical functions might include resetting the printer to factory-default settings, changing to compressed print, setting the margins for printing, or selecting a font. A complete list of printer functions and the command codes to invoke them is usually given in the back of the printer technical manual.

Print Device Modes

A print mode is a collection of functions that will set up the printer to carry out a specific task such as printing sideways on envelopes. Default print devices usually have several print modes that might include options like "Landscape Compressed Print" or "Letter Portrait, 66 lpp, 12 cpi." The network manager can combine printer functions to create new printer modes.

Forms

If you use preprinted forms, letterhead, or envelopes in a network printer, you may wish to define a Netware form for each of them. Each special form is assigned a form name and number other than 0. Netware uses the form number associated with a print job to allow the operator to change forms before the job is printed.

Using Print Devices, Modes, and Forms

Once print devices, modes, and forms have been established, they can be incorporated into your print jobs. The easiest way to do this is to run PRINTCON and create print job configurations that specify the appropriate form, print device, and mode. Each print configurations can be given a name, such as *LJ_Landscape*, and copied to the user's configuration directories. The user can invoke the configuration using the format:

```
CAPTURE J=<print job configuration name>
```

For example:

```
CAPTURE J=LJ_Landscape
```

If a mode is included in the configuration, the setup commands will be sent to the printer immediately before the print job. If the print job configuration specifies a form other than the form that is currently in use, the job will not print until the print queue operator has indicated to the print server that the new form has been loaded.

Form Changes

The network manager can configure the printer to handle a form change in a number of ways. The procedure is specified under the "Queue Service Mode" line of the printer configuration section of PCONSOLE. The default service mode is "Change forms as needed," which will print all jobs in the established order. In this case, whenever a job that calls for a different form is encountered, the queue is stopped, a message is sent to the users and groups on the printer "notify list," and the printer waits until the form has been changed. Another option is to "Minimize form changes across queues." In this case, the print server rearranges the print order so that all jobs specifying the current form are printed first. When the job with a different form is ready to be printed, a message is sent to a list of users and/or groups. This "notify list" is specified for each printer using PCONSOLE. The job is held until the Print Server operator indicates that the form has been changed. This can be done using the Print Server Information/Print Server Status/Control menu on PRINTCON.

The Print Server Command (PSC) Utility

The **PSC** command utility can quickly send a command to a printer. For example, PSC can be used to inform the print server that the form has been changed on a printer. In particular, if the job requires form #1 and is to be printed on printer #0 of print server Willow, the command is:

```
PSC PS=Willow P=0 MO=1
```

where **MO** is an abbreviation for MOUNT FORM. You can set up a default value for the print server (**PS**) and the printer number (**P**) using the DOS SET command in the form:

    SET PSC=PSWillow P0

Once this has been done, you can abbreviate the above PSC command to

    PSC MO=1

The PSC utility can be used to quickly stop and start a network printer. For the following example, assume you have set up the PSC variable to designate a default server and queue. If the printer jams and you need to quickly stop the queue, you can issue the command:

    PSC STO K

where **STO** is an abbreviation for STOP (the printer) and **K** is an abbreviation for KEEP (the current print job in the queue). Later, when the printer jam has been cleared, you can issue the command:

    PSC START

and the queue will resume at the beginning of the last print job. Most PSC command functions can also be carried out using the PCONSOLE menu utility.

Note *The previous discussion applies only if you are using a print server. If you are using Netware 2 core printing, all printer notification messages appear at the file server console and the print form is changed using the console PRINTER (P) command. For example, notify print services that form 1 has been mounted on printer 0 using the command*

    :P 0 FORM 1

Similarly, the printer can be controlled by entering commands like

    :P 0 STOP, *and* :P 0 START

Using the SPOOL Command

Use the console command :**SPOOL** 0 <queue name> to designate a default print queue. The default queue is used with NPRINT or CAPTURE when no queue is designated. This also assigns a printer number to the queue. SPOOL is required for some older network-aware applications that use network printer numbers (such as WordPerfect 4.2). This same command works on all versions of Netware.

Automating Server Configuration Using AUTOEXEC.NCF

On a Netware server, the **AUTOEXEC.NCF** file is analogous to the DOS AUTOEXEC.BAT file. It executes when a Netware 3 or 4 file server is started and can contain commands to start server processes, set parameters, and load NLMs. For example, the AUTOEXEC.NCF file can name the server, set up disk and network interface cards, and start up a print server. AUTOEXEC.NCF is normally created when Netware is installed on the server and can be modified using INSTALL.NLM or edited with a text editor. Here are some statements from a typical AUTOEXEC.NCF file:

```
FILE SERVER SCREAMER
IPX INTERNAL NET 111
MOUNT ALL
LOAD SITELOCK
LOAD 3C503 PORT=300 INT=3
BIND IPX TO 3C503 NET=22
LOAD PSERVER WILLOW
LOAD MONITOR
```

In this case, the file server name is SCREAMER and it uses an internal network address of 111 (hex). With MOUNT ALL, the disk drives are made available to users, and then SITELOCK, a third-party Netware loadable module (NLM), is loaded. Next, the 3Com 3C503 network interface card is set up and connected to the outside world as network 22 (hex) running the native Netware IPX protocol. This server uses PSERVER.NLM for print services using the print server named WILLOW. The last command loads the MONITOR utility that can be used to display network information on the server console.

Summary

Setting up network print services often involves the following steps:

→ Connecting the printers

→ Creating print queues

→ Creating a print server

→ Defining the printers

→ Associating queues with printers

→ Starting the print server

→ Loading RPRINTER for remote printers

The network manager can automate the startup process using the AUTOEXEC.NCF file at the file server and the AUTOEXEC.BAT file at a dedicated print server or a remote printer.

There are several steps to ensure that a print job is printed in a specific mode and/or on a special form. These may include:

→ Using PRINTDEF to define a form

→ Using PRINTDEF to define a device and mode

→ Using PRINTCON to define a print job (this may specify a form, device, and/or mode)

→ Using CAPTURE J=<jobname> to direct output from the PC application to the network queue, with the form, device, and/or mode as specified in the print job configuration

The PSC command can be used to quickly carry out a number of printer control functions. Most of these can also be accomplished using the PCONSOLE menu utility.

Review Questions

* **1.** Describe two ways that you could associate a network print queue with local port 2 (LPT2:).

* **2.** Who is the print queue operator, by default, when a queue is first created? Who are the default queue users?

3. What are the steps required to set up a print server?

Exercises

1. Refer to the example at the end of the section on setting up core printing. Draw a diagram showing the printers and print queues that are set up. Your diagram should illustrate that one printer serves more than one queue.

2. Describe how you might set up a printer serving two queues with different priorities. How would this be useful if you had some print jobs that require a special form in the printer?

3. Can a network print queue be assigned to local port 2 (LPT2:) if the local workstation does not have a second parallel port? How would you set this up?

4. Printers can be attached directly to the serial and parallel ports of the print server. What is the maximum number of printers that can be attached in this way?

Key Terms and Commands

AUTOEXEC.NCF

Core printing

Device

Form

Function

Mode

NPRINTER

Print command

Print server

PRINTDEF

PSC

PSERVER

Queue operator

Queue user

Remote printer

RPRINTER

SPOOL

Unit 18 **Additional Security Issues**

As organizations "downsize," they are turning to networks in increasing numbers. Many networks run mission-critical applications and handle data that may be sensitive or confidential. This trend will accelerate as networks become more powerful and reliable.

We have seen that Netware offers a host of features to aid the network administrator in setting up a network environment that is both easy to use and secure. As networks become more important to an organization, the security aspects often outweigh other factors. This unit covers some additional security issues, focusing on the Netware 3 or 4 file server.

Learning Objectives

At the completion of this unit, you should be able to

1. understand the most important network security issues,
2. describe the threat posed by computer viruses,
3. outline some of the security precautions that can be taken with a Netware server,
4. understand the additional security available with Netware 4.

Console Security

Many things can be accomplished at the file server console, including some that can disrupt a network. These can range from simply turning the server off at the wrong time, to loading programs that can permit an unauthorized user to gain access to supervisory accounts. Therefore, it is wise to take additional security precautions to prevent tampering.

The most effective precaution is to limit physical access to the file server. If you have a secure area, it is usually advisable to locate the file server there. Although the location may be out of the way, you can use the Novell **remote console** utility **RCONSOLE** to access the server console from your network workstation, and can move printers to a convenient location using RPRINTER or NPRINTER. If you use RCONSOLE, it is a good idea to load MONITOR on the server and set a keyboard password to lock the keyboard. (It can be unlocked either locally or, if using RCONSOLE, by entering the keyboard password or the SUPERVISOR password.)

You may wish to take two other precautions to prevent tampering with the file server: Use a hardware power-on password at the server, and employ the :SECURE CONSOLE command.

Many servers allow you to set a **hardware password** that must be entered whenever the server is powered on. Setting a hardware password on the file server prevents an unauthorized user from starting the system and booting from a floppy disk to load a program that can read and modify the netware disk.

The **SECURE CONSOLE** command does a number of things to prevent tampering. It prevents the loading of NLMs from a floppy drive or drive C:, so an intruder cannot load a "trojan horse" module. It also forces you to power the server down to restart it. This forces the use of the hardware password before the server can be restarted.

Other precautions at the server might include:

➡ Locking the case and/or the keyboard with a key lock

➡ Using MONITOR.NLM to establish a software keyboard lock

➡ Booting the server from a floppy disk and locking the floppy in a safe place

The SECURITY Utility

The Netware **SECURITY** utility is a tool that the network manager should run periodically to check for possible security holes. It reports all users with insecure or no passwords, users who have SUPERVISOR rights, and users who have been granted excessive network privileges. This is a good way to catch potential problems before they happen and may be the easiest way to detect users who are security-equivalent to SUPERVISOR. The SECURITY program is located in the SYSTEM directory on the server.

Viruses

Networks can be vulnerable to computer **viruses**. Fortunately, there are several good virus-checking programs available. These include third-party solutions like VIREX and Sitelock, as well as shareware programs that can be obtained from bulletin boards. In addition, newer operating systems like DOS 6 include additional virus-prevention features.

In any case, the first line of defense is to establish a secure network environment. Ensure that programs are virus-free before installing them and, once installed, FLAG all program files as read-only to help prevent contamination of the network.

Backups

Establishing and enforcing a regular schedule of backups is perhaps the most important security precaution you can take. A carefully planned backup strategy can help avoid disaster in the event of virus contamination, fire or water damage, sabotage, or equipment failure. Your backup rotation should be set up with these possible disasters in mind. In particular, it is a good idea to maintain off-site archives that go back at least six months, to ensure that the network manager has the capability of restoring an uncontaminated version of a program or file.

Additional Security Features of Netware 4

Netware 4 has a number of additional security features. We have already mentioned the Netware Directory Services (NDS) that provides another layer of security. Other security features range from a sophisticated **authentication** system that prevents unauthorized "eavesdropping" on the network, to an **auditing** feature that allows an independent investigation of all changes to the network configuration.

Authentication operates in the background to ensure that passwords are protected, to verify that messages originated from the sender, and to prevent modification of the message as it passes across the network.

The auditing feature allows the network administrator to set up a special auditor account. The auditor account has no supervisory capabilities, but cannot be accessed by the network supervisor, and has full access to a database that records all supervisory operations. This provides a supervisory oversight capability without interfering with the functions of the network manager.

Another security feature of Netware 4 allows the network supervisor to have any username and password. In particular, you need not have a network manager named SUPERVISOR, and, in fact, the default supervisor name is ADMIN.

These features give Netware 4 a higher security rating than earlier versions.

Summary

As networking becomes more central to the mission of an organization, security becomes of greater concern. Netware can provide an extremely secure environment. However, an improperly configured and casually maintained network can permit security breaches.

It is wise for the network manager to take every available security precaution. A careful set of security measures together with a solid backup strategy can avoid a potential disaster or the loss of sensitive data.

Review Questions

* **1.** List at least three measures that can be taken to improve the security of a Netware file server.

2. What is the purpose of the SECURITY program?

* **3.** What is the single most important security precaution you can take?

4. What are the additional security features of Netware 4?

Exercises

1. Assume that you back up your file server onto a set of tapes. Design a backup rotation where:

  a. You make a new backup tape every day and the most recent five daily backups are always available.

  b. You set aside a weekly backup and the most recent four weekly backups are always available.

  c. You set aside a monthly backup and the most recent 12 month's backups are always available.

  How many sets of tape would it take to implement your strategy?

2. Contact a computer software retailer to determine the most popular virus prevention software. Will this software work in a network environment?

3. Contact a network manager to determine how important security is in his or her environment. See if he or she can describe any security problems that have been encountered.

Key Terms

Auditing

Authentication

Hardware password

RCONSOLE

Remote console

SECURE CONSOLE

SECURITY

Virus

Conclusion

Netware is a solid product that is increasingly being used as the basis of the small-business corporate computing strategy. The most recent version, Netware 4, provides an evolving set of additional features that position it as an enterprise-wide solution for the larger business.

New generations of software are providing formidable challenges to Netware's dominant market position. More powerful operating systems like Windows NT, and revised versions of UNIX, including Novell's UNIVEL, provide multitasking systems with network capabilities built in. A trend toward the adoption and development of open networking standards like TCP/IP may give an advantage to the UNIX systems that provide powerful graphical interfaces and have well-integrated TCP/IP capabilities.

As graphics-based systems like the Macintosh and UNIX workstations make inroads into the business world, there is likely to be a convergence of all network systems toward standards that will allow diverse systems to work together. Novell has taken some steps to support standard networking protocols such as TCP/IP and standard messaging protocols such X.400. This is especially true for Netware 4. However, it is not clear at this point if Netware 4 can provide enough features to keep network planners from jumping to other systems.

Nor is it clear whether Netware can maintain its dominant market position. Computer experts and the stock market seem to forecast that Novell is likely to remain a strong force. The continued success of Novell may depend on how well it can satisfy the increasingly diverse needs for universal connectivity.

Appendix A **Glossary**

3270 The generic name for a family of IBM system components—terminals, printers, terminal cluster controllers, and mainframe front-end processors—that can be used to communicate with a mainframe using the SNA protocol. All of these components have four-number names, some of which begin with the digits 327.

802.x A generic term that refers to the work and the standards promulgated by an Institute of Electrical and Electronics Engineers (IEEE) committee. The 802.x standards describe the wiring, signaling, topologies, and access schemes for a number of network products at the physical and data-link layers of the OSI model. 802.3 describes the cabling and signaling for a system nearly identical to classic Ethernet and its derivative, Starlan. 802.5 describes IBM's Token Ring architecture.

Access protocol (or Media Access Control [MAC] protocol) The rules that LAN workstations abide by to avoid "traffic jams" when sending signals over network wiring. The most common protocols are Carrier Sense Multiple Access (CSMA) used by Starlan and Ethernet and token passing used by Token Ring, MAP, and others.

Acoustic coupler An almost outmoded type of data communications device with sound transducers that connect to a telephone handset for the purpose of data transmission.

Adapter board A hardware enhancement that plugs into a bus or connector on a computer. Network adapters include interface cards that allow the computer to connect to a network (for example, Ethernet adapter).

AFP (Appletalk Filing Protocol) Allows file sharing in a Macintosh environment.

Analog signal This is a signal that is continuously variable as opposed to a digital signal that has discrete levels.

ANSI (American National Standards Institute) A standards-setting body with members from more than 900 companies and 200 consumer and professional organizations. ANSI is the U.S. representative to the ISO.

API (Application Programming Interface) A standard set of tools that allows an application to gain access to distributed system resources. Committees are working to establish uniform standards for APIs.

APPC (Advanced Program-to-Program Communications) This IBM protocol is analogous to the OSI model's sessions layer, in that it enables application programs to send data to each other through the network.

AppleShare A network operating system that uses the AFP and runs on a dedicated Macintosh server. It also includes software for Macintosh workstations. Netware for Macintosh includes the AppleShare server features and also includes the software for the workstations.

AppleTalk A set of protocols analogous to SPX/IPX used on an AppleShare network.

Application layer The highest (seventh) layer of the OSI model. It defines the way that application programs interact with the network operating system.

ARCnet (Attached Resources Computing Network) A proprietary networking architecture running at 2.5Mbps using a token-passing bus configuration. It supports coaxial cable in both a star and bus configuration as well as twisted pair and fiber optics. It has been widely used and is highly regarded by many installers for good reliability and performance. (It has been described as the VW Beetle of networks.) Recent progress has been hampered by advances in other alternatives and the fact that it is not an IEEE standard.

ARPANET A packet-switching network sponsored by the U.S. Department of Defense. It uses the TCP/IP protocols.

ASCII (American Standard Code for Information Interchange) (pronounced *as-key*) This is the data alphabet used to encode letters, numbers, and other characters as seven-bit numbers on IBM PCs and other computers.

Asynchronous A method of unsynchronized "serial" data transmission between two computers that allows characters to be sent one bit at a time at irregular intervals. This is usually done by preceding each character with a "start" bit and following it with a "stop" bit. The IBM serial port uses the RS-232 asynchronous protocol.

Attach Usually refers to establishing a connection to a file server.

Attributes Describes properties of an entity such as a file or a directory. File attributes include Read-Only, Sharable, and Execute-Only. Directory attributes include Read, Write, and Create.

Bandwidth (1) The range or band of frequencies used by a communications signal; (2) The possible band of frequencies that can be carried by a communications channel. In this case the bandwidth limits are imposed by the physical medium— the wires, or other devices such as amplifiers. A bandwidth is usually given in hertz (Hz), representing the difference between the highest frequency and the lowest frequency in the band.

Baseband A transmission technique in which only one signal occupies the medium (*compare* broadband).

Baud rate   A measure of the speed of a data communications line referring to the number of discrete signal events per second. The baud rate differs from bits per second when there are start, stop, or other signal bits present.

BIOS (Basic Input/Output System)   A set of programs built into DOS computers that enables the CPU to communicate with drives, keyboards, displays, printers, and other attached input and output devices.

Bisync (Bisynchronous Communications [BSC])   This refers to one of the two commonly used methods of encoding data for synchronized transmission between devices in computer systems. Data characters are gathered into a "frame" and marked by two synchronization bits. *Also see* SDLC, asynchronous.

Bit rate   A measure of transmission speed expressed in units of bits per second (bps), thousands of bits per second (Kbps), or millions of bits per second (Mbps).

BPS   *See* **Bit rate**.

Bridge   A link between similar local area networks (at the OSI network layer), which enables users on one network to use all the resources available on the other.

Broadband   A medium that is set up to provide many different frequency bands for different signals. The MAP protocol and the first IBM PC network use broadband signals on coaxial cable.

Buffered repeater   A device that amplifies and regenerates signals so that they can travel farther along a cable. This type of repeater also controls the flow of messages to prevent collisions.

Bus   A wiring arrangement or topology in which all network stations receive the same messages at roughly the same time.

Cache   This refers to a block of high-speed memory to which a computer or communications device can have rapid access. Netware uses directory caching where disk information is stored in RAM to provide quick access.

Carrier   The basic signal that is used to transmit data. The carrier is modified or "modulated" by the data signal before being transmitted.

CCITT (Consultative Committee on International Telephone and Telegraph)   A standards-setting organization based in Geneva, Switzerland, that is involved with setting standards associated with OSI (*compare* X.25 and X.400).

CICS (Customer Information Control System)   This software from IBM runs on mainframe computers and makes a variety of services available for application programs. It furnishes easy ways for programs to enter and request data in mainframe files.

Cluster controller   A computer that sits between a group of terminals and an IBM or similar mainframe computer, gathering messages and "clustering" them for more efficient transmission.

Coax or coaxial cable   A type of wiring commonly used for Ethernet and other networks. Coaxial cable contains a copper inner conductor surrounded by plastic insulation and then a woven copper or foil shield.

Collision Detection   *See* **CSMA**.

Concentrator   An intelligent device that combines data from several devices on one circuit.

CPU   The central processing unit of a computer.

CSMA (Carrier Sense Multiple Access)   A protocol for sharing a common bus. Stations listen to the network media and transmit only if the cable is not is use. CSMA is usually combined with a means of detecting a "collision" when two stations begin to transmit at the same time. This leads to the acronym CSMA/CD, which stands for CSMA with Collision Detection.

Data link layer   The second layer of the OSI model, which has to do with the flow of data to and from network devices and methods to ensure that the data arrives safely.

Data terminal equipment   *See* **DTE**.

DCE (Data Communications Equipment)   Usually refers to a standard scheme for wiring the 25-pin asynchronous connector on a modem or other communications device.

DECnet   A set of proprietary networking protocols from Digital Equipment Corporation (DEC). These protocols are being merged with the OSI standard and will be available as DECnet Phase V.

DFS (Distributed File System)   This is a high-level network protocol that is designed to allow computers on a network to use the files and peripherals of another networked computer as if they were local.

Digital signal   A sequence of binary numbers, or 0s and 1s, that electrically have two states, on or off, generated by a computer or similar device.

DTE (Data Terminal Equipment)   Usually refers to a standard scheme for wiring the 25-pin asynchronous connector on a terminal, printer, or other communications device. This configuration is used on the IBM PC serial communications port.

EBCDIC (Extended Binary Coded Decimal Interchange Code)   This is the scheme used to encode the alphabet and other characters on IBM mainframe systems. This uses a different coding scheme from the more commonly used ASCII code.

Ethernet   A widely used network cable and access protocol scheme originally developed by Xerox, and now marketed by DEC, 3Com, and others.

EtherTalk   AppleTalk packets encapsulated to run on an Ethernet network.

FAT (File Allocation Table)   A hidden table on a floppy or hard disk that keeps track of the physical location of files in terms of the block numbers on the disk.

FDDI (Fiber Distributed Data Interface)   An emerging standard for a high-speed (100Mbps) medium for LAN and other data connections over fiber optics.

Fiber optics   A data transmission method that uses light pulses sent over glass cables. Fiber is available in several diameters, but the size with a 62.5-micron core and 125-micron glass covering appears to be emerging as a standard (*compare* FDDI).

File lock   *See* **locking**.

File server   A type of server that holds files in private and shared subdirectories for LAN users. *See also* server.

Frame   A packet on a Token Ring network.

Front-end processor (FEP)   A computer that sits between groups of cluster controllers and the mainframe computer, concentrating signals before they are transmitted to the mainframe.

FTAM   The ISO File Transfer Access Method.

FTP   The Department of Defense File Transfer Protocol.

Gateway   A shared portal between dissimilar networks. Often used to connect PCs to a larger information resource such as a large packet-switched (X.25) information network or a mainframe computer.

Gigabyte (GB)   A unit of measure for memory or disk storage capacity consisting of a thousand megabytes (MB) or a billion bytes.

Handshaking   Exchange of codes and signals between two computer devices to ensure that equipment is ready to communicate.

HLDLC (High-Level Data Link Control)   Communications protocol used for synchronous connection to X.25 packet-switched networks. Similar to SDLC.

IDE   The Integrated Drive Electronics is a standard interface for hard disks.

IEEE (Institute of Electrical and Electronics Engineers)   Establishes standards for wiring and network protocols on the physical and data-link layers of the OSI model.

IEEE 802.x standards   *See* **802.x.**

Interface   A hardware and/or software connection between devices that satisfies a set of rules for common interconnection and signal exchange.

Internetwork   A system of two or more networks that are connected by a router.

IPX (Internetwork Packet Exchange)   A subset of the XNS protocols used by Novell in Netware that allows the exchange of message packets on an internetwork.

ISDN (Integrated Services Digital Network)   An international standard for digital communications over standard telephone lines.

ISO   The International Standards Organization (in Paris), which developed the Open System Interconnection (OSI) model.

Kbps   *See* **bit rate**.

Local area network (LAN)   A collection of two or more computers, usually housed within a single building or cluster of buildings, that are connected in such a way as to permit the sharing of data, software programs, and resources such as printers and storage devices.

Locking   This refers to the process of closing a file or data record to prevent access by another user. This is necessary if more than one person has access to the data (via the network) and ensures that only one user can change it at any one time.

Logical Unit (LU)   Terminal emulation application in an IBM SNA environment. Some types of LUs can communicate with each other (LU 6.0, 6.1, or 6.2).

Login script   A set of instructions that are automatically carried out when a user logs into a network. Analogous to the AUTOEXEC.BAT file in DOS.

MAC (Media Access Control)   *See* **access protocol**.

MAP (Manufacturing Automation Protocol)   A LAN specification using a token-passing protocol over a broadband bus. This network scheme was designed by an industry group led by General Motors to provide real-time process control features. It has been adopted as the 802.4 Token Bus standard.

Mbps   *See* **bit rate**.

Media   The cabling or wiring used to carry network signals. Typical examples are coax, fiber optics, and twisted pair wire.

Media Access Control (MAC)   *See* **access protocol**.

Megabyte (MB)   A unit of measure for memory or disk storage consisting of approximately one million bytes.

MHS (Message Handling Service)   A set of protocols for sending electronic mail over local area networks. MHS has been adopted by Novell and a number of other vendors including Ashton-Tate and WordPerfect.

MIPS (millions of instructions per second)   A measure of the processing speed of a computer.

Modem   A contraction of MOdulation/DEModulation. A device for converting digital signals to analog for transmission on a telephone system and for reconverting them to digital at the receiving end for input to a machine.

Multiplex   To interleave or send more than two messages on the same channel.

NDS (Netware Directory Services)   A distributed, replicated, hierarchical database that is the central concept of the Netware 4 operating system. NDS contains information about all resources on the network and is patterned after the X.500 standard.

NetBIOS (Network Basic Input/Output System)   A network software standard originally developed by IBM and Sytek for the original PC Network. It has since been adopted by a number of third parties as a standard for communications between workstations on a network at the session layer. These vendors either provide a version of NetBIOS to interface with their hardware or emulate its session-layer communications services in their network products.

NetView   IBM's proprietary network monitoring and management software for SNA networks.

Network adapter, network interface board   *See* **adapter**.

Network layer   The third layer of the OSI model, containing the logic and rules that determine the path to be taken by data flowing through a network. A network bridge operates on this layer.

NFS (Network File System)   A distributed file system protocol that allows computers on a network to use the files and peripherals of another networked computer as if they were local. This protocol was originally developed by Sun Microsystems but it has been placed in the public domain and has been adopted by a number of other vendors.

NLM (Netware Loadable Module)   Software that can be incorporated into the Netware 3 or 4 operating system.

OSI (Open Systems Interconnection)   A generic model that divides the working of a network into seven layers, each with a specific protocol. Its aim is to provide compatibility in communications among the products of different vendors.

Packet   A unit of data sent over a network. Packets usually include the identities of the sending and receiving stations, error-control information, and data.

Packet switching   A technique for sending information over wide-area communications networks that breaks messages into data "packets." Each packet has an address and information that allows the information to be reassembled at the other end. X.25 is a commonly used protocol for packet-switching networks.

PAD (Packet Assembler/Disassembler)   A device used to prepare packets for transmission and/or to reassemble received packets using an X.25 packet-switching network.

Parity   This refers to a system for checking transmission errors in which an extra "parity" bit is added to transmitted data. The parity bit is chosen so that each transmitted character always has an odd number of ones (odd parity) or always has an even number of ones (even parity).

PBX (Private branch exchange)   This refers to telephone switching equipment that serves a site. The equipment is usually privately owned or leased and connected to the local public telephone system. A digital PBX or PABX (Private Automated Branch Exchange), is a computerized switch that can also handle data as well as voice transmission.

Peer-to-peer resource sharing   A software architecture that lets any station contribute resources to a network while still running local application programs.

Physical layer   The first layer of the OSI model. It consists of network wiring and cable.

Point-to-point   A virtual or logical connection between two computers.

Polling   A method of resource sharing by which the host computer samples each line at periodic intervals to determine when devices are ready to transmit data.

Presentation layer   The sixth layer of the OSI model, which formats data for screen presentation and translates incompatible file formats.

Print server   A network device (usually a computer) that makes one or more attached printers available to other users. The print server usually requires memory and/or a hard disk to store or "spool" the print jobs while they wait to be printed. The print jobs are stored in a print queue, which determines the order in which they are printed.

Pentium   The code name for Intel's 586 processor family.

Protocol suite   A set of rules for communications intended to provide orderly transmission between stations on a data link.

RAM (random access memory)   System memory used in a computer.

Record lock   *See* **Locking**.

Redirector   Software loaded into a PC network workstation to capture and "redirect" operating system requests for file access or printing services when these files or printing services are located at the server. The end result is that the files and/or printers are available to the application as if they were locally attached.

Repeater   A device that amplifies and regenerates signals so they can travel farther on a cable.

RFS (Remote File System)   A distributed file system protocol that allows one computer to use the files and peripherals of another as if they were local. This scheme is based on a high-level network protocol called Streams developed by AT&T as a part of UNIX V.

Rights   Netware security feature that controls to which directories and files a user has access. Rights are assigned by the network supervisor.

Ring   This refers to a network topology where each computer is linked in series with all of the others. This topology usually includes a means to bypass a computer to avoid breaks when a computer goes down.

Router   An intelligent device that connects two or more networks and moves packets from one network to another based on the destination of the packets. Netware servers can perform routing functions between dissimilar types of network hardware.

RS-232   The signaling scheme used on the serial port of the IBM PC and other devices. *Also see* **asynchronous**, **DTE**, **DCE**.

SAA (Systems Application Architecture)   A set of specifications written by IBM describing how users, application programs, and communications programs interface. SAA represents an attempt to standardize the look and feel of applications.

SDLC (Synchronous Data Link Control)   An essential part of IBM's networking architecture SNA. SDLC is more efficient than the older bisynchronous protocol in terms of packaging data for transmission between computers. With SDLC, packets of data are sent over the line without synchronization or other signal bits.

Server   A computer on a network that makes file, print, or communications services available to other network stations.

Session   Usually refers to a connection between two devices for the purpose of carrying out a task. The term can also refer to a connection between a PC emulating a mainframe terminal and the mainframe itself.

Session layer   The fifth layer of the OSI model, which sets up the conditions whereby stations on the network can communicate or send data to each other. Network gateways operate on this level.

Shell   The network program that is loaded onto the workstation and allows it to communicate with the network server.

SMB (Server Message Block)   A distributed file system network protocol, used in conjunction with DOS Redirector and NetBIOS, that allows one computer to use the files and peripherals of another as if they were local. Developed by IBM and Microsoft and adopted by many other vendors.

SMTP   The Department of Defense's Simple Mail Transfer Protocol. Usually associated with TCP/IP.

SNA (Systems Network Architecture)   IBM's scheme for connecting its computerized products so that they can communicate and/or share data.

SNMP (Simple Network Management Protocol)   An application-level protocol that provides the capability to send and receive network management data. Operates over UDP.

SPX (Sequenced Packet Exchange)   Operates on the transport layer to ensure delivery and to assemble packets in the correct sequence. Uses IPX to deliver the messages across a Novell network.

Star   Describing a wiring topology in which each end user is connected by a dedicated wire to a central host or control node.

Starlan   A networking system developed by AT&T that uses CSMA protocols on a twisted pair telephone wire. A subset of 802.3.

Streams   A high-level protocol that enables easy development of applications sharing data or resources across a network. The protocol was developed by AT&T and is incorporated into UNIX system V (Release 3) and later versions.

Synchronous   A type of data transmission in which the computers involved share the same timing. *Compare* asynchronous.

T1   This is a common scheme for multiplexing (combining) several signals onto one channel that transmits data at 1.544Mbps. The configuration provides for 24 channels, each with a data rate of 56Kbps along with 8Kbps of signaling and control.

TCP/IP (Transmission Control Program/Internet Program)   A set of protocols promoted by the Department of Defense that is used for wide-area and local-area networks, to link dissimilar computers across large networks. TCP runs at the transport layer, while IP runs at the network layer and is usually used on networks with Ethernet at the data link and hardware layers.

Token bus   Refers to a token-passing network that uses a linear bus configuration. *See* **ARCnet** and **MAP**.

Token passing   A transmission protocol in which a control packet or token circulates from one station to the next on a network, to determine an orderly sequence for data transmission. After one station sends a message, the token is passed to the next one, which is then allowed to transmit.

Token Ring   Refers to the wire and the access protocol scheme promoted by IBM. Network stations are arranged in a logical ring and pass information from one to the next. This architecture is described in the IEEE 802.3 standard.

Topology   The way stations or nodes in a network are connected. The physical topology refers to the wiring of the system, and the logical topology refers to how signals flow in the network.

Transparent   Not apparent to the user.

Transport layer   The fourth layer of the OSI model. Software in this layer checks the integrity of and formats the data (1) carried by the physical layer, (2) managed by the data layer, and (3) perhaps routed by the network layer.

Tree   A topology with multiple branching connections arranged in a layered hierarchy and emanating from a single point (root).

Twisted pair   A transmission medium consisting of a pair of wires twisted around each other (at six turns per inch) and encased in a sheath. Some telephone wire is twisted pair.

UDP (User Datagram Protocol)   Provides a connectionless service for the exchange of messages between hosts. Operates on the same level as TCP but does not ensure reliability. It thus demands less overhead and is simpler to implement.

UNIX   A multiuser, multitasking operating system developed by Bell Labs and used in a wide variety of computer systems.

UPS (Uninterruptible Power Supply)   A backup power unit that uses batteries to provide temporary power in the event of a power outage.

UPS monitoring   A feature that can be installed on a network server to automatically monitor the status of the power input to the UPS and shut the server down after a preset time without normal power.

Virus   A program that can replicate by attaching itself to other programs. Viruses often attach to DOS system files and can cause loss of data or corruption of program files.

VTAM (Virtual Telecommunications Access Method)   This software runs on IBM or compatible mainframe computers and works with the Network Control Program to establish communications between the host and the cluster controllers.

VTP   The ISO Virtual Terminal Protocol.

Wide area network (WAN)   A network that connects devices that are geographically dispersed, usually located in different buildings, and more than a kilometer or so apart.

Wideband   This refers to the bandwidth of the connection. A wideband connection can handle high-speed transmission between devices and is often used to link devices that need to transmit large amounts of data.

Workstation   Any individual personal computer. Usually implies that the computer is connected to a network.

X.25   A CCITT standard that describes how data is handled in a packet-switched network.

X.75   A standard for internetwork gateways.

X.400   A CCITT standard for messaging and document distribution that, if widely adopted, could lead to a global electronic mail network.

X.500   A developing standard for addressing and providing electronic "directory assistance" services for wide-area electronic mail systems. NDS is patterned after the X.500 model.

XNS (Xerox Network Services)   A multilayer protocol developed by Xerox for its Ethernet network. The protocols have been adopted, at least in part, by Novell and other vendors for use in their network schemes. XNS allows network stations to use files and peripherals located elsewhere on the network as if they were local.

Appendix B **Answers to Selected Review Questions**

1-3.

    a. NIC—Network Interface Card.

    b. WAN—Wide-Area Network.

    c. Hub—Wiring center or network junction box.

2-1.

    a. Read-write capability—CD ROM is read-only, WORM is a write-once system, and a hard disk is read-write.

    b. Speed—a CD ROM and a WORM drive are much slower to read than a hard disk (by a factor of 10 or more). Writing to a WORM drive is very much slower than writing to a hard disk (by a factor of 20 or more).

    c. Storage capacity—each CD ROM stores about 600MB, while a WORM drive stores 150–600MB depending on the manufacturer. You can change the disks on a CD ROM or a WORM drive, so the total storage capacity is unlimited. A hard disk has a fixed storage capacity ranging from 40MB to 1,300MB or more.

2-2. For a file server, the emphasis is usually on speed, RAM, hard disk storage capacity, and durability/reliability. There is no need for a color VGA monitor, a mouse, or user software.

2-3. Factors related to networks might include built-in network hardware and hard disk storage capacity. In particular, networking built into the system could be cost-effective and more efficient (faster), while a network system may not need so much hard disk storage capacity as compared with a stand-alone system. Other important factors include processing speed, memory, type of display adapter and monitor, footprint, and type of keyboard.

3-2. The FORMAT command prepares a disk for use. You would want to format a hard disk (the C: drive) only when the system is installed. In many cases, systems come already formatted with software installed on the hard disk. In this case you would never want to format the C: drive.

4-1. The commands that are necessary depend on the workstation setup. Netware 2 and 3 often use IPX/NETX. In this case, the commands include IPX and NETX. If the ODI workstation files are in use (Netware 3) use LSL, <hardware mlid>, IPXODI, and NETX. If the VLM workstation files are in use (Netware 4) use LSL <hardware mlid>, IPXODI, VLM. In this case, the workstation installation program will set up a batch file called STARTNET to automate this process. Finally, once the appropriate shell files are loaded, use **F:** and **LOGIN** to begin the login process. For example, if you are using the 3COM Etherlink II network card (3C503), use one of the following series of commands to initially start the network:

IPX:	ODI:	VLM (STARTNET):
IPX	LSL	LSL
NETX	3C503	3C503
F:	IPXODI	IPXODI
LOGIN	NETX	VLM
	F:	F:
	LOGIN	LOGIN

4-3.

a. Set up the computer to operate as a DOS machine.

b. Check jumpers and install the network interface card. Run setup program (if appropriate) to configure the NIC.

c. Copy the appropriate workstation files to the boot device. This includes either the hardware-specific ODI driver (3C503, NE2000, or similar file provided by the manufacturer) or the IPX file that includes the appropriate hardware settings.

d. Set up or modify the AUTOEXEC.BAT file to load the appropriate network files (see 4-1).

e. Set up or modify CONFIG.SYS to ensure that other devices do not conflict with the network interface card. You may need to add an exclude command to the EMM386 driver that blocks out high memory used by the NIC. For example, if the network card is using 16KB at D0000, add **x=D000-D4FF** to the EMM386 command.

f. Test the setup. If the system hangs, or can't find a server, check to ensure that there are no conflicts with interrupts or high memory.

5-1. The 802.x standards govern how bits are moved around on a network. They fit into the lower group. The IPXODI program fits into the middle third (at the network layer). (IPX can also be regarded as fitting into the middle third. However, it contains hardware-specific information and overlaps into the Data Link layer.)

5-2. 10Base-T differs from standard Ethernet primarily in the way the signal is encoded on the wire and the type of wiring used (twisted-pair vs. coaxial).

6-1. Twisted pair.

6-2. IBM Cabling System—IBM

DECconnect—DEC

Premises Distribution System—AT&T

6-3. Fiber optics are appropriate to interconnect and electrically isolate different buildings or if one or more of the following conditions is present:

➡ Very long distances between stations (more than 500 meters).

➡ Very high network traffic (more than 10Mbps).

6-4. Plenum wire is constructed to be able to withstand high temperatures. It is required when wire is strung without a conduit in ventilation ducts, walls, or over suspended ceilings or near work areas. It is not used all the time because it typically costs two or more times as much as standard wire.

7-2. The two use different cable types, topologies, and have different costs. Ethernet uses coaxial cable, bus topology, and costs slightly less than 10Base-T, which uses twisted pair and a star topology. In addition, distance limitations are different. 10Base-T stations must be no more than 100 meters from the hub, while thin Ethernet can span at least 185 meters, and thick Ethernet can span 500 meters.

7-3. The social protocol analogous to CSMA/CD is "listen attentively and don't speak when someone else is speaking."

8-2. The distance between one PC and the next is important because this is the distance that the signal has to be sent before being retransmitted. This distance will determine the total losses in the line.

8-3. 300 meters.

8-4. The microphone analogy is inaccurate for a number of reasons: Talking into the microphone broadcasts the message, while a Token Ring sends the message from one station directly to the next around the ring. There are no priorities in the analogy. There is no method of acknowledgement in the analogy. And so on.

9-1. 93 ohm coaxial cable.

9-2. Token Passing Protocol.

9-3. 256.

10-1. Both connect two or more network segments and retime the signal before placing it on the other segment. However, a repeater retransmits all packets without looking at addresses, while a bridge looks at the destination address and does not retransmit if it is recognized to be a "local" packet.

10-3. Repeater, bridge, router, gateway.

10-5. Because of the relatively slow transmission speed capabilities of the telephone system.

11-2. Once the network software is loaded onto your workstation, the login process is begun by changing to the network drive (usually F:) and typing **LOGIN**. If you got a response "Bad command or filename," this indicates that the system could not find the LOGIN program located in the \LOGIN directory on the file server. This might happen because you are not connected to the file server or have selected the wrong drive letter. This could also indicate that the network shell program has not been loaded.

11-3. Both types of drives behave in much the same way as far as DOS is concerned. Differences include: G: is a pointer to a network drive, not a physical drive, and therefore can change from one session to another; G: can be set up make a subdirectory look like the root directory; and two network drives (say G: and H:) can point to the same network directory.

11-4. The CAPTURE command configures your computer to print to a network printer or queue. CAPTURE can be used with or without parameters. If no parameters are specified, the system default parameters are used. If you have defined a default print job configuration using PRINT-CON, then the queue and print job configuration parameters specified by the default configuration are used.

Thus, the default print job configuration you set up using PRINT-CON determines the print configuration that you get when you type **CAPTURE**.

12-2. Menu utilities are used as follows:

SESSION*	Sets up and views drive mappings and other parameters associated with the user session.
FILER	Manages files and directories. This includes viewing the contents of directories and copying or deleting files and directories.
VOLINFO	Displays the status of the network volumes.
SYSCON*	Manages the system. This includes setting or viewing the properties of users and groups and setting up login scripts.
FCONSOLE*	Views and manages certain aspects of the file server. This includes viewing and clearing connections to the server, setting the server date and time, and shutting down the server.

PCONSOLE	Views and manages print servers, printers, and queues.
PRINTCON	Views and manages print job configurations.
PRINTDEF	Views and manages print forms, print devices, and printer setup commands.

*With Netware 4, the SESSION utility has been replaced by NETUSER and the windows-based NWUSER, the SYSCON utility has been replaced by NETADMIN and the windows-based NWADMIN, and the FCONSOLE utility has been eliminated. (All console management is done through the MONITOR.NLM utility.)

12-3. The user login script can be used to customize the individual user's environment at each login.

13-1. Jobs of a typical network manager may include: setting up users and groups, installing hardware and software, creating backups, and solving network problems.

13-4. Groups can assist the manager in setting up the network environment and making it easy to maintain.

14-1. The login password is the most common access restriction. Others might include station or time restrictions, intruder detection, and account expiration.

14-3. Read-Only/Read-Write and Sharable/non-sharable.

14-4. The effective rights are the same as the explicit rights given.

15-2. The default login script is executed if there is no user login script. This can be bypassed using the EXIT command (or the NO_DEFAULT command of Netware 4).

15-3. The percent sign is used at the beginning of an identifier such as LOGIN_NAME that appears within quotes in a WRITE statement.

15-4. An IF statement can be used in a login script to conditionally execute login commands. Conditions might include MEMBER OF "<group name>" or P_STATION="<station address>".

16-2. FLAG the files as Read-only.

17-1. Use CAPTURE with /L=2 or use PRINTCON to set up a configuration that specifies local port #2.

17-2. By default, the print queue operator is the SUPERVISOR that set up the queue and all users in the group EVERYONE are print queue users.

18-1. Lock up the server, install a server hardware password, and use SECURE CONSOLE.

18-3. Assuming you have a reasonably well-managed network environment (with passwords, groups, access restrictions, and so on) the single most important security precaution is to create regular backups.

Index

Notes

Notes

Notes

Notes

Notes